JUSTICE, EQUALITY AND CONSTRUCTIVISM

T0341345

Ratio Book Series

Each book in the series is devoted to a philosophical topic of particular contemporary interest, and features invited contributions from leading authorities in the chosen field.

Volumes published so far:

Wittgenstein and Reason, edited by John Preston
Contributions by Jacques Bouveresse, Hans-Johann Glock, Jane Heal, Genia Schönbaumsfeld, Severin Schroeder, Joachim Schulte and Crispin Wright.   ISBN 978-1-4051-8095-5

The Meaning of Theism, edited by John Cottingham
Contributions by Sir Anthony Kenny, Alvin Platinga, John Haldane, Richard Norman, David Benatar, Michael McGhee and John Cottingham.   ISBN 978-1-4051-5960-9

Metaphysics in Science, edited by Alice Drewery
Contributions by Brian Ellis, Stathis Psillos, John Heil, Stephen Mumford and Alexander Bird.   ISBN 978-1-4051-4514-5

The Self?, edited by Galen Strawson
Contributions by Barry Dainton, Ingmar Persson, Marya Schechtman, Bas C. van Fraassen and Peter van Inwagen.   ISBN 978-1-4051-2987-9

On What We Owe to Each Other, edited by Philip Stratton-Lake
Cotributions by Onora O'Neill, Jonathan Wolff, Joseph Raz, Derek Parfit, Mark Timmons and T. M. Scanlon.   ISBN 978-1-4051-1921-4

The Philosophy of Body, edited by Mike Proudfoot
Contributions by Quassim Cassam, Maximilian de Gaynesford, Alison Adam, Sean Dorrance Kelly, Hubert L. Dreyfus, Iris Marion Young and Michael Brearley.   ISBN 978-1-4051-0895-9

Meaning and Representation, edited by Emma Borg
Contributors: John Hyman, Gregory McCulloch, Tim Crane, Jerry Fodor, Ernie Lepore, Paul Horwich and R. M. Sainsbury.
ISBN 978-0-631-23577-4

Arguing with Derrida, edited by Simon Glendinning
Contributors: Geoffrey Bennington, A. W. Moore, Thomas Baldwin, Stephen Mulhall and Darren Sheppard.   ISBN 978-0-631-22652-9

Normativity, edited by Jonathan Dancy
Contributors: Peter Railton, Joseph Raz, Christopher Hookway, John Broome, Frank Jackson and John Skorupski.   ISBN 978-0-631-22041-1

JUSTICE, EQUALITY AND CONSTRUCTIVISM

Essays on G. A. Cohen's *Rescuing Justice and Equality*

Edited by
BRIAN FELTHAM

A John Wiley & Sons, Ltd., Publication

This edition first published 2009
Originally published as Volume 21, Issue 4 of *Ratio*
Chapters © 2009 The Authors
Book compilation © 2009 Blackwell Publishing Ltd

Blackwell Publishing was acquired by John Wiley & Sons in February 2007. Blackwell's publishing program has been merged with Wiley's global Scientific, Technical, and Medical business to form Wiley-Blackwell.

Registered Office
John Wiley & Sons Ltd, The Atrium, Southern Gate, Chichester, West Sussex, PO19 8SQ, United Kingdom

Editorial Offices
350 Main Street, Malden, MA 02148-5020, USA
9600 Garsington Road, Oxford, OX4 2DQ, UK
The Atrium, Southern Gate, Chichester, West Sussex, PO19 8SQ, UK

For details of our global editorial offices, for customer services, and for information about how to apply for permission to reuse the copyright material in this book please see our website at www.wiley.com/wiley-blackwell.

The right of Brian Feltham to be identified as the author of the editorial material in this work has been asserted in accordance with the Copyright, Designs and Patents Act 1988.

Wiley also publishes its books in a variety of electronic formats. Some content that appears in print may not be available in electronic books.

Designations used by companies to distinguish their products are often claimed as trademarks. All brand names and product names used in this book are trade names, service marks, trademarks or registered trademarks of their respective owners. The publisher is not associated with any product or vendor mentioned in this book. This publication is designed to provide accurate and authoritative information in regard to the subject matter covered. It is sold on the understanding that the publisher is not engaged in rendering professional services. If professional advice or other expert assistance is required, the services of a competent professional should be sought.

Library of Congress Cataloging-in-Publication Data

Justice, equality and constructivism : essays on G. A. Cohen's Rescuing justice and equality / edited by Brian Feltham.
    p. cm. – (Ratio book series) (Ratio special issues)
"Originally published as Volume 21, Issue 4 of Ratio."
Includes bibliographical references and index.
ISBN 978-1-4051-9175-3 (pbk. : alk. paper)
    1. Cohen, G. A. (Gerald Allan), 1941– Rescuing justice and equality.   2. Equality.   3. Social justice.   I. Feltham, Brian.
    HM821.C65J87 2009
    305.01–dc22

                                                                                    2009005782

A catalogue record for this book is available from the British Library.

Set in 11 on 12 pt New Baskerville by SNP Best-set Typesetter Ltd., Hong Kong

01 2009

CONTENTS

NOTES ON CONTRIBUTORS

Richard J. Arneson is Professor of Philosophy at the University of California, San Diego. He has published numerous papers including work on luck egalitarianism.

Will Braynen is studying at the University of Arizona, working on his PhD in political philosophy and cognitive science. He has published papers on prejudice and game theory.

Thomas Christiano is Professor of Philosophy and Law at the University of Arizona. His many publications include his latest book *The Constitution of Equality: Democratic Authority and Its Limits* (Oxford University Press, 2008).

Brian Feltham lectures on philosophy and political theory at the University of Reading. He has published papers on political legitimacy and value disagreement.

Kasper Lippert-Rasmussen is Professor of Political Theory at the University of Aarhus. He has published papers on ethics and political philosophy as well as editing *Egalitarianism* (Oxford University Press, 2006) (co-edited with Nils Holtug).

Michael Otsuka is Professor of Philosophy at University College London. His publications on moral and political philosophy include *Libertarianism without Inequality* (Oxford University Press, 2003).

Thomas Pogge is Leitner Professor of Philosophy and International Affairs at Yale University. His publications include *Politics as Usual: What Lies behind the Pro-Poor Rhetoric* (Polity Press, 2009).

Andrew Williams is Professor of Philosophy at the University of Warwick. He is co-editor (with Matthew Clayton) of the *Ideal of Equality* (Macmillan, 2000) and an Associate Editor of *Politics, Philosophy and Economics*.

ACKNOWLEDGEMENTS

The chapters in this collection also appear in a special issue of the journal *Ratio* (Vol. XXI, No. 4, December 2008). Earlier versions of a number of the chapters were presented at a one-day *Ratio* conference at the University of Reading on 21 April 2007. The subsequent production of the collection was aided by, not least, the care and diligence of all of the contributors. Additional thanks belong to *Ratio*'s editor, John Cottingham, as well as Jacqueline Scott and Sharon Low at Wiley-Blackwell; Mike Otsuka for keeping us up to date with drafts of Cohen's book; Thomas Pogge for his astuteness on matters of pagination; and, for her generous and speedy assistance regarding details of the final version of Cohen's work, Phoebe Kosman at Harvard University Press. Very special thanks should go to G. A. Cohen for his support, for his stimulating work, and not least for his coming to the conference in April to do his best to persuade us why he is, after all, quite right. Andrew Williams deserves the recognition and my considerable gratitude for setting up this project to begin with; without his initial vision and planning, many of these essays might not even exist and none of them would exist in their present form. Finally, my personal thanks go to my friend and frequent advisor, Véronique Munoz-Dardé: for all those little things and the big things for which one turns to one's friends.

Brian Feltham

1

INTRODUCTION

Brian Feltham

G. A. Cohen has an amazing and richly rewarding body of work behind him already. As an interpreter of socialist, and especially Marxist, ideas into the vernacular of contemporary analytic political philosophy he is second to none. As a critic of mainstream theoretical liberalism he has been a welcome voice, urging us to consider the importance of solidarity, of the significance of social justice to our personal choices, as well as the simple and ancient thought that justice is (in some way) equality first and foremost – on this view, anything else said about justice is either finesse or compromise. Whether or not they share his views on all these points, liberal egalitarians cannot afford to ignore them. Among his many topics, one of Cohen's most sustained targets is the work of John Rawls: a thinker whose reflections on justice start with a concern for the fair treatment of people who are considered as equals, yet who ends by endorsing inequalities – albeit only if this makes everyone better off.[1] Surely, Cohen encourages us to think, if no other mistake has been made, Rawls must at least have changed the subject. Justice can't suborn inequality, can it?

In his new book, *Rescuing Justice and Equality*,[2] G. A. Cohen pays Rawls an enormous compliment. And not just in the section he entitles '*The Greatness of John Rawls*', where Cohen goes so far as to suggest that, in all the history of Western political philosophy, only two books might be said to be greater than Rawls's *A Theory of Justice* (those two being Plato's *Republic* and Hobbes's *Leviathan*; mighty company indeed). In fact, the whole of Cohen's book, and much of Cohen's earlier work, is a form of compliment to Rawls. Cohen has been one of the most valuable and persistent critics of the Rawlsian project, and he has been so not as someone who denies Rawls's achievements, but as someone who recognises what

---

[1] Although it is, of course, making the worst off better off which is singled out in the statement of Rawls's difference principle.
[2] G. A. Cohen, *Rescuing Justice and Equality* (Cambridge, Mass.: Harvard University Press, 2008).

many of us find so attractive and so compelling in this fairness-based, left-leaning vision of liberalism. While the state is seen as a framework in which to live out our different life-choices, Rawls sees our political relationships not as limited to the pursuit of our separate and several self-interests, but as also conditioned by a concern and respect for all who attempt to pursue happiness within the limits of a due concern for others. Moreover, we want to lead our lives in a society of equals and not indifferent to the disadvantages of others. We want to be reasonable, to be just. Without this sense of the appeal of Rawls's aims, Cohen would not be so insightful and – in the best, positive way – provocative a critic as he is.

What he shares with Rawls is a concern with equality and a fairer society. He is also minded to agree, albeit for his own reasons, that there are limits to how involved we want the state to get in our everyday lives. Perhaps as importantly (and in distinction from most conservative critics), Cohen shares something of the theoretical ambitions of much of liberalism. By reflecting on our ideals, it is to be hoped we can form true opinions about how we should be living – however far that may be from our current practices. This needn't imply utopianism, but just a healthy sense that, whatever justice is, we may be at some considerable remove yet from living justly (and, with Cohen's approach, perhaps even at some remove from being able to live justly). When Cohen makes a plea for solidarity and for justice to be seen as personal, guiding our individual life choices as well as the regulation of our political institutions, he does so as, in key ways, almost a fellow traveller (although the shared journey in this case is that of left-wing political theory rather than Marxism).

Fellow traveller or no, Cohen has serious disagreements with the Rawlsian project. Much of Cohen's value as a critic of Rawls however, depends less on his respect for his target than the precise distance and direction in which he stands from it. Cohen is not a liberal. Not that he is illiberal, by any means. But he approaches liberalism very much from the left, and is moved principally by variations on socialist (and socialist anarchist) ideas and concerns. Two of his major disagreements with liberalism are summarised in the very title of the book that forms the focus of this collection. Cohen wants to rescue justice and equality from the Rawlsian project. In regards to equality, Cohen thinks that Rawls starts from a set of assumptions that tell in favour of understanding justice as equality but then, illicitly, smuggles in other concerns that lead him to conclude that justice requires something rather different. In particular, Cohen charges that Rawls's version of the difference principle – which permits inequalities that favour the worst off – permits too much inequality and for the wrong, non-justice related, reasons. Thus, in aiming to rescue equality, Cohen wants to argue that Rawls should have preferred something more wholeheartedly egalitarian. In particular, if justice directs us to make the worst off as well off as possible, why stop until no-one has more than the worst off (who are now also the equal best off along with everyone else)?

Also to be rescued is the concept of justice itself – or, as we might say, the purity of the concept of justice, untrammelled and uncompromised by concerns (moral or otherwise) that properly belong under a different heading. Rawls's constructivist process aims to explain what is just in terms of a range of concerns, including practicalities and other matters of (non-value) fact. For Rawls, it counts against a theory of justice that it is practically unachievable. Cohen, by contrast, aims to show that the question of justice is separate from practical, factual questions. Practicality is affected by a range of considerations, not least amongst which are psychological, motivational factors. We might ask ourselves what, given our psychological tendencies, is just for us; but on Cohen's view we will find that we can answer this (if we can) only because of a prior commitment to what is just independent of these facts – since there must be some principle marking out the justice-related significance of these psychological tendencies. If psychology affects what is just, it is only because justice first comments on psychology. Fundamentally, justice is not conditioned by facts; and for this reason Rawls was never really offering a theory of *justice* at all. If, for reasons of practicality, or of stability, or of efficiency, we settle for the Rawlsian state, we may well be settling for something both different to and less than a perfectly just society.

Cohen's book is densely argued, with much Rawlsian exegesis that is as carefully considered as it is inventively inspired. The brief summary here of Cohen's concerns is only a hint at the complexity and appeal of his critique. This collection of essays is in large part an attempt to pay to Cohen something of the compliment he has paid to so many others, and to Rawls especially. That is, the compliment of carefully argued disagreement. These responses are not exclusively Rawlsian, but do show an appreciation of the significance of Rawls's work, as well as of Cohen's deeply thought criticisms of it. In the essays by Arneson, Christiano and Braynen, and Lippert-Rasmussen, Cohen is challenged on his position about the intimate relationship between justice and equality. Arneson denies that Rawls makes an illicit move away from an initial commitment to equality, while Lippert-Rasmussen deftly explores the space left for justified incentives on both Rawls's and Cohen's views. Christiano and Braynen even offer something of a synthesis between Cohen and Rawls, one which holds that equality is required by justice, but claims that some inequalities – those which offer superior benefits to the worst off – are less unjust than others, and even less unjust than some equal distributions. Otsuka seeks to provide a better explanation of why we don't want the state to have too much detailed control over our individual life-choices, one which is centred on self-ownership rather than Cohen's concern with invasiveness. Pogge criticises Cohen's understanding of fundamental moral principles, including justice, as being fact-insensitive. He aims to clarify what Cohen has in mind while arguing that Cohen fails to argue successfully against all relevant rival views. Lastly, Williams attempts to defuse some of Cohen's criticisms of Rawls's constructivism, particularly Rawls's crucial restriction of his difference principle to the basic structure of society rather than to our more personal economic decisions.

G. A. Cohen has inspired so many of us with his sense of the great importance of even abstract questions of justice, his dedication to rigorous critical analysis and his love of carefully laid out, logical argumentation. No less has he inspired us with the sheer pleasure he takes in what, in his hands, becomes a far from dry and impersonal subject matter. It is a great pleasure and privilege to be connected with this collection of essays on Cohen's latest book, *Rescuing Justice and Equality*, a book with which he makes a major contribution both to Rawlsian scholarship and to political and moral philosophy quite generally.

2

JUSTICE IS NOT EQUALITY

Richard J. Arneson

Abstract

This essay disputes G. A. Cohen's claim that John Rawls's argument for the difference principle involves an argument from moral arbitrariness to equality and then an illicit move away from equality. Moreover, the claim that an argument from moral arbitrariness establishes equality as the essential distributive justice ideal is found wanting.

Rescuing Justice and Equality is an original, subtle, and astute work of ethical and political philosophy.[1] From its justly renowned author, G. A. Cohen, we have come to expect no less. The work ranges over questions of ethical theory (metaethics) and normative political theory. My remarks address only the latter.

Cohen's book tries to develop both a sustained critique of some ideas on justice that had been affirmed by John Rawls[2] and a meditation on the ideal of socialism. This dual aim does not as one might fear force a split personality on the enterprise, which in fact shows a unified theme. Cohen interprets John Rawls as the quintessential liberal, urging that egalitarian justice can in principle be fully attained in a market economy setting. More important to Cohen is the way he sees Rawls distinguishing between public and private life in the just society. For Rawls, justice is a norm that mainly regulates the structure of major institutions – the basic structure of society. Individuals are bound by justice mainly to support just institutions when they exist or help bring them about when they do not, and to obey laws compatible with justice. Within just institutions, individuals are morally free to carry out their own projects and aims. This picture of the just society conjures up for Cohen the image of an economy in which

---

[1] G. A. Cohen, *Rescuing Justice and Equality* (Cambridge, MA and London, England: Harvard University Press, 2008). (Further references to this work will be enclosed in parentheses in the text.)

[2] See John Rawls, *A Theory of Justice*, rev. ed. (Cambridge: Cambridge University Press, 1999).

selfish individuals try to do as well for themselves as they can within the just institutional rules. The image is defective, says Cohen, and the defect precludes our calling a society that fits the image a just society.

According to Cohen, the distributive justice component of social justice requires that the distribution of benefits and burdens across individual persons is fair, and bringing about and sustaining the just distribution are the responsibilities of the individual members of society not merely the standard for choice of basic structural institutions. In Cohen's idea of a just society individuals make their choices in daily life, within the limits of an appropriate personal prerogative that each of us has to pursue her own projects and aims, with a view to contributing to the good of others and to bringing about a just distribution, which Cohen supposes to be roughly an equal distribution. The shape and structure of institutions must also satisfy principles of justice, but that's not enough. In this connection one might compare the just society and the society that overcomes racism. To qualify as non-racist, it is not enough that a society's institutional rules should prevent people from acting on racial prejudice when they interact within basic institutions.

I am entirely in agreement with Cohen that whether or not a society qualifies as ideally just depends not merely on the structure of its institutions but also on the dispositions and conduct of its members. Cohen's way of pressing this point against Rawls achieves a deep insight. One might put part of Cohen's point this way: in the ideally just society, the dispositions and conduct of the members, within the constraint of the personal prerogative accorded to each individual to give extra weight to her personal concerns in deciding how to live, do not limit the degree to which the society fulfills the goal set by the justice standard. People's dispositions are set so that they maximize the degree to which justice goals are fulfilled. (Notice that this leaves it open to what extent individuals should be motivated in daily life by concern for the common good versus concern for their private good. Perhaps beyond a certain point, being concerned to improve the lives of others may be counterproductive. It is even abstractly possible that each person's being disposed to care only for himself and those near and dear to him would, in conjunction with a matching best set of institutions, be maximally conducive to the achievement of justice goals.) Cohen stresses a claim that goes further: in the just society, each member embraces the ideal of social justice as a goal and is dedicated to conducting her life so as to secure and maintain it (modulo the personal prerogative). There is an attitudinal component of the just society: a common devotion to the common good. That the members of society have this attitude is according to Cohen an intrinsic component of justice not merely a good instrument for achieving justice.

One might wonder how any of this is relevant to a meditation on socialism. One might suppose that the socialist following Jean-Jacques Rousseau takes 'men as they are and laws as they might be'[3] and proposes public ownership of a society's productive resources as the best social arrangement under these constraints. If you instead take people as they ideally ought to be and basic institutions as they ideally ought to be you are engaged in what Rawls pejoratively calls the 'ethics of creation'.[4] Cohen disagrees. He thinks that what is just is what is ideally fair. What is ideally fair in given circumstances depends on what those circumstances actually are. What would be ideally fair if humans could secrete manna from their fingertips is not relevant. But to discover what is ideally fair one should abstract from any limits in people's willingness to comply with fairness constraints or to promote fairness goals. So if equality turns out to be ideally fair, it remains so even if we humans are so constituted that we are bound to act against this norm. According to Cohen equality or something close to it (equal access to advantage) does turn out to be ideally fair upon reflection, and the essence of socialism is the idea of a society that achieves this equality ideal and whose members are dedicated to it. Cohen is of the opinion that institutions and culture and individual will can shape motives, so socialist equality may also be feasible, but it would remain ideally fair even if it were motivationally out of reach.

If we then relax the constraint of assuming that humans will go along with what is ideally fair, we then get a series of hard questions centering on the issue, what is the best we can get to from where we are now. The best place we can get to is the place in which all our values properly weighed, not only our justice values, are maximally realized. If we are deontologists and accept moral constraints, we may want to amend the question: what is the

<hr />

[3] Jean-Jacques Rousseau, *On the Social Contract, or Principles of Political Right* [1762], in Rousseau, Donald Cress, ed., *The Basic Political Writings* (Indianapolis: Hackett Publishing, 1987), p. 141.

[4] Rawls, *A Theory of Justice*, p. 137.

best place we can get to, without violating moral constraints we should accept, from where we are now.

From this standpoint, the Rawlsian enterprise can now be seen to have strayed off-track in two important ways. Rawls the liberal supposes that social justice is a norm that regulates primarily institutions and only secondarily individuals (the general secondary requirement is to support acceptable institutions and comply with their rules). On the contrary, Cohen sees distributive justice as a set of principles that specifies a fair distribution of benefits and burdens, good and bad fortune, to individuals, and holds that one who accepts such principles must see them as normative both as to what institutional arrangements she should support and what courses of action she should choose. Rawls the theorist identifies what is just with principles that would be chosen by persons who were trying by this very choice of principles to produce the best outcomes for themselves under constraints that assure impartial choice. But this preliminary formulation, to be later refined and developed in further discussion, already makes a big mistake in Cohen's view. Rawls according to Cohen also veers off-track in a second way: People situated in a Rawlsian original position will choose with a view to gaining better outcomes, but that postulated motivation blends concern for fairness with concern for values that have nothing to do with fairness (but that would go into an assessment of outcomes all things considered).

I have already expressed agreement with Cohen on his first critical claim. However, his second critical claim is dubious. Whether or not the Rawlsian original position construction helps to characterize the best conception of social justice (or the best conception of the narrower ideal of distributive justice), a characterization even of the narrower ideal does not go astray just in virtue of assuming that the justice of a distribution of resources depends in part on the extent to which that distribution, compared to alternatives, improves the outcome by improving the quality of people's lives. Even if you thought equality were a big component of justice, why think it's everything?

Against incentives

Cohen frames his critique of Rawls as a critique of liberal justifications of capitalism. The starting point of these justifications is the idea of an equality-versus-efficiency tradeoff. Economic equality, though desirable in itself, is a drag on economic productivity. A market economy is assumed to be an engine of economic productivity, but tends to generate inequality in people's condition, especially over the long run, as effects of early random shifts ramify and grow. If we reasonably care about both equality and efficiency (productivity), we should uphold a market economy modified by redistributive regulation and taxation and transfer, up to the point indicated by the correct tradeoff ratio. So runs the justification.

From this standpoint, Rawls's position might appear to be maximally egalitarian. The difference principle in its leximin formulation asserts that (within the limits established by lexically prior principles of justice) the basic structure of society should be set so that it maximizes, as a first priority, the advantage level of the worst off person, then as a second priority, the advantage level of the second worst off person, and so on, up to the best off.[5] One could not tilt more strongly in favor of benefiting the worst off than by adopting the difference principle.

Cohen demurs, in two ways. He observes that if inequality, generated by incentive payments offered to talented persons to induce them to work productively, would work to maximize the position of the worst off, there is in principle another equally productive possibility: the talented work at their most productive employment and forego the incentive payment. In this scenario their productivity gains are shared equally across all members of society. If all members of society are committed to egalitarian principles, and guide their economic choices by them, then no incentive inducements are needed to sustain productivity, and the equality-versus-efficiency tradeoff disappears, or rather, is no longer a binding constraint on the pursuit of equality. Moreover, the society in which individuals are regulated by egalitarian principles in their daily economic choices as well as in their choice of basic structure institutions is a more just society than one in which only the latter choice is so regulated. (The moral requirement to aim at the greater fulfillment of social justice goals in one's daily economic choices is understood by Cohen to be limited by an appropriate personal prerogative.)

The upshot is that according to Cohen a society that is through and through just, just in the disposition of its members as well

---

[5] On leximin, see Amartya Sen, 'Rawls versus Bentham: an axiomatic examination of the pure distribution problem,' *Theory and Decision*, 4 (1974), pp. 301–310.

as in the shape of its basic social structure, will not display incentive-generated inequality (modulo the prerogative).

Suppose that people are not through and through just and we are thrust back in the realm of nonideal theory. The equality-versus-efficiency tradeoff then reappears. Let us say that the aggregate sum of advantages can be increased if inequality is instituted. Perhaps we should institute some inequality – this depends on further factors. A particularly uncontroversial case occurs if we can make someone better off without thereby making anyone else worse off. The Pareto norm then says we should move to some position against which this complaint cannot be made. Satisfying Pareto, we create inequality. Cohen insists that we should not now say that inequality is recommended by distributive justice. Distributive justice, he affirms, continues to favor equality. We have a conflict of values, and although no doubt in some cases the aggregative and efficiency norms should be followed, we should not misdescribe this choice as one that involves no sacrifice of distributive justice.

Cohen accuses Rawls of failing to call things by their right names here. Rawls affirms the difference principle as a principle of distributive justice, but this affirmation confounds the true egalitarian principle of distributive justice with the nonjustice considerations that compete with it and that sometimes outweigh it and determine what we ought to do all things considered. The Rawlsian mix-up facilitates our viewing a capitalist economy, when and if it would be justified by the difference principle, as fully satisfying the principles of distributive justice, but viewing things this way is wrong and glosses over a genuine unredeemed loss. The mistake here is the same in character as the one we would make if, finding in some unfortunate social circumstances that slavery cannot be abolished without generating unacceptable moral costs, we described the situation, in which all things considered we should not act to eliminate slavery here and now, as one in which slavery is just.

On Cohen's view, the Rawlsian mistake is especially poignant, as we see when we notice following Cohen that Rawls's intuitive argument for the difference principle is incoherent. Rawls advances an argument from moral arbitrariness that establishes equality of a certain sort as uniquely what distributive justice calls for. Rawls then asserts a nonjustice value, the Pareto norm, and claims that we are driven by that value to abandon the presumption of equality established by the moral arbitrariness argument and to embrace as our ultimate distributive justice value the difference principle, which says in effect, do the best we can for the worst off, and pay no heed whatsoever to equality of condition as per se morally valuable. An egalitarian argument leads to equality and then somehow incongruously lurches past it, pushed by some other value entirely, and the principle we then end up with is identified with distributive justice rather than as a compromise with distributive justice or as a counterconsideration. So urges Cohen.

Conceptions of justice

I shall argue that Cohen is wrong to find in Rawls's intuitive argument for the difference principle an incoherent lurch past insistence on equality of condition. I shall also examine from several angles Cohen's rendering of the argument from moral arbitrariness that is supposed to establish a strong presumption in favor of equality. The argument does not look good from any angle.

Even though we find in Cohen's discussions no good argument for the claim that distributive justice demands equality, the claim might nonetheless be correct. However, this is doubtful. My own view is that the fundamental moral principle governing distribution and all other justice matters is to be found in the family of prioritarian principles, which say that one ought morally always to implement an act or policy, among the alternatives, that would produce no less moral value than anything else one might have done instead, moral value being entirely a function of well-being that accrues to individuals.[6] (The moral value of achieving a gain in well-being for an individual is greater, the greater its size, and greater, the lower the person's lifetime well-being level would be absent this benefit, and greater, the more deserving the individual.) Priority versus Cohen-style equality involves a consequentialism versus deontology issue that is irrelevant for purposes of this discussion. Setting that issue aside, one can construe priority as the idea that distributive justice is beneficence weighted by

---

[6]   On priority, see Derek Parfit, 'Equality or Priority?', reprinted in Matthew Clayton and Andrew Williams, eds., *The Ideal of Equality* (New York: Macmillan and St. Martin's Press, 2000).

priority that varies depending on how badly off one is – this idea might be set in a deontological frame with its paraphernalia of constraints and options. Cohen clearly rejects this idea, and I have no arguments for it, so this side of the discussion ends in a standoff. It's an odd standoff, seemingly more verbal than substantive. Cohen insists that distributive justice demands equality, but allows that other justice considerations might militate against equality, and allows also that nonjustice moral considerations including aggregative welfarist considerations might militate against the lot of justice considerations, and perhaps rightly outweigh them. He is opposed to priority in the sense that he does not declare a commitment to it, and not in the sense that he declares a commitment against it. His substantive claim is that priority, along with the Rawlsian difference principle and other moral riffraff, should not usurp the name of *justice*.

It might seem tedious and fruitless to quarrel with a theorist about the names she attaches to the entities that concern her. Nonetheless I do want to quarrel with Cohen on this point. I object to his definitional stipulations regarding the term *justice*. Something, though perhaps not much, is at stake here. It is perhaps worth mentioning that Cohen does not regard himself as making a convenient definitional stipulation; he is asserting what he regards 'our' conception of justice to be.

In ordinary English usage the term 'justice' tends to be applied to what the speaker regards as a paramount value and also an all-things-considered value. My dictionary ready to hand gives as the first meaning for the 'justice' entry the following: 'moral rightness, equity.' On this usage, if something is not morally right, it's not just. John Rawls appeals to something like this usage in the magisterial first sentences of *A Theory of Justice*. 'Justice is the first virtue of social institutions, as truth is of systems of thought. A theory however elegant and economical must be rejected or revised if it is untrue; likewise laws and institutions no matter how efficient and well-arranged must be reformed or abolished if they are unjust. Each person possesses an inviolability founded on justice that even the welfare of society as a whole cannot override.'[7] Rawls starts with the formal point, that justice is the paramount value in social relations, and then couples it with the

---

[7]   Rawls, *A Theory of Justice*, p. 3.

polemical claim that justice, the trumping value, has nothing to do with the maximization of welfare.

Back in 1861 John Stuart Mill had in effect protested against the move that Rawls is making.[8] Mill more or less asserts that in a narrow sense of the term *justice*, it might be counterposed to anything that smacks of utility-maximizing, but there is also a broad sense of the term, perhaps more common, according to which it is an all-things-considered and hence paramount moral evaluation of social matters. It is illegitimate to slide between the narrow and broad senses to convey the impression that obviously justice broadly conceived has nothing to do with utility. On the contrary, says Mill, even those who take equality to be the essence of the ideal of justice, end up adjusting the ideal so that inequalities that are expedient are not deemed unjust, nor are equalities that are inexpedient deemed to be just.

I'm with Mill up to a point. When judgments invoke the idea of justice as a trumping value, it is also an all-things-considered value, and it is a wide open question, to what extent increasing aggregate human well-being is a consideration included in the calculation. I would go further. When justice is identified with equality, it is equality of treatment that is in play, and the notion of equality here is formal, that people who are in relevant respects the same should be treated the same. Any ideal of substantive justice appeals to fairness, and it is part of our idea of fairness that if a resource is worth a lot to you and a little to me, you should get it (I would add that how badly off each of us would otherwise be is also a factor). 'Be reasonable!' you might say if I act as a dog in the manger, hogging a resource that does hardly anything for me when the cow really needs it to get fed. 'Be fair!' you might just as well say in that situation.[9] Cohen asserts that when we are talking specifically about *distributive justice*, whether a distribution is just depends on what one person gets as compared with what others get, and the operative notion of justice here is equality, nothing except differential fault or choice or desert serving to justify inequality. I simply report that I don't find in my own convictions any trace of this supposed ideal of distributive justice; nor do I

---

[8]   J. S. Mill, *Utilitarianism* [1861], George Sher, ed. (Indianapolis, Hackett Publishing, 1979), chapter 5, paragraph 10.
[9]   The non-dog-in-manger principle should surely be incorporated in any plausible interpretation of the ideal of socialism. On the principle, see Brian Barry, *The Liberal Theory of Justice* (Oxford: Oxford University Press, 1973).

see that it is derivable from more basic common-sense convictions we should be loathe to relinquish.

Cohen might wish to argue in a revisionary spirit that we ought to accept his distributive ideal, but it would be misleading to claim any entitlement much less exclusive entitlement to the word 'justice' with its powerful connotations. I suggest it would make for clarity if he used a fresh invented term for his ideal, say *distributive jarstice*. Then a reader like me could register that he does not care at all for distributive jarstice without thereby seeming to insinuate that he cares not at all for the paramount all-things-considered value in social relations, or not at all for the more specific value of fairness in social relations.[10]

Cohen objects that Rawls plays fast and loose with the notion of *distributive justice* when he allows that, with other principles in place, a distribution of resources that satisfies the difference principle is just, fully accords with the conception of distributive justice that we ought to accept. The difference principle in one of its formulations says that an inequality in resource shares is just provided that it works to maximize the set of resources (primary social goods) that goes to the worst off. Cohen proposes to identify distributive justice with luck egalitarianism.

Equality and moral meritocracy

Some regard the canonical statement of luck egalitarianism to be this formulation introduced by luck egalitarian Larry Temkin: 'It is bad (unjust and unfair) for some to be worse off than others through no fault [or choice] of their own.' Call this the Temkin formulation (it's from his book *Inequality*).[11] Cohen affirms roughly the same view, when he avows his conviction 'that an unequal distribution whose inequality cannot be vindicated by some choice or fault or desert on the part of (some of) the

---

[10] But isn't the prioritarian being equally revisionary in denying that it matters at all (except instrumentally) from the standpoint of justice, how one person's condition compares to the condition of others? My point is simply that Cohen cannot appeal to any uncontroversial common notion to buttress his claim that distributive justice essentially requires equality.

[11] Larry Temkin, *Inequality* (Oxford: Oxford University Press, 1993), p. 13. In footnote 21 on the same page he adds to his formulation the words 'or choice' that I have added in square brackets.

relevant affected agents is unfair, and therefore *pro tanto* unjust, and that nothing can remove that particular injustice' (p. 7).

And some might regard this as a necessary supplement to this canonical statement of luck egalitarianism: 'It is morally bad (unjust and unfair) if some have less than others beyond the level of inequality that is proportionate to the comparative merit (faultiness) of their choices.' Unless you add the supplement, or something along this line, your luck egalitarian principles set no limit on how much worse off than another it is acceptable for a person to be, given that she has behaved in a manner that is more faulty, even by a smidgeon, than the other person or persons with whom her condition is being compared.

The Temkin formulation looks to be unpromising as a canonical statement of any sort of egalitarianism, because it is ambiguous. It is (can be interpreted as) fully compatible with the following: 'It is morally bad (unjust and unfair) if some have the same as others through no merit of their own.' This says it is morally bad if some make less meritorious, more faulty choices than others yet end up with the same as what others get. And both the Temkin formulation and the just-stated claim can be read as partial statements of moral meritocracy. The full statement of moral meritocracy would be: 'Each person should get good fortune in life according to her moral merit (the degree to which her choices are faulty, compared to others' choices)'. (This is not quite right, because the Temkin formulation includes an odd causal requirement – whether inequalities are good or bad depends on the causal process through which the inequality arises. My statements of moral meritocracy extrude the odd causal requirement.) Interpreted as a partial statement of moral meritocracy, Temkin's supposedly canonical statement of luck egalitarianism affirms no sort of egalitarianism at all. I don't claim this is the only possible way to read his statement of principle – I claim it is ambiguous.

To get any sort of egalitarianism unambiguously into the picture, you need to amend or interpret the Temkin formulation so it tilts in favor of equal distribution in some way: Perhaps it might be read as asserting: Equality is morally desirable, provided that inequality does not arise through fault or choice. (This is neutral on the issue, what is desirable when inequality does arise through fault or choice.) Another possibility: Add to the Temkin formulation a straight affirmation of equality: It is morally better if all have the same. Another possible view is that equality is morally desirable only provided the equal desert condition obtains, and it is morally desirable that the equal desert condition obtains.

Cohen versus Rawls

Cohen argues that Rawls produces an intuitive argument for the difference principle that illicitly moves from (a) premises that appeal to the value of equality to (b) a conclusion that affirms the difference principle as the core principle of distributive justice. However, the difference principle, most clearly in its leximin formulation, attributes no value whatsoever to equality. According to the leximin difference principle, justice requires (against a background of equal basic liberty and fair equality of opportunity) that as a first priority, the primary goods allocation going to the person with least primary goods be maximized, then as a second priority, the primary goods allocation going to the second-worst off person be maximized, and so on up to the best-off person. In other words, the difference principle instructs us to arrange the basic social structure so as to make the worst off as well off as possible, and to let the equality chips fall where they may. Cohen protests that there is an incoherence in this argument. From premises affirming the intrinsic moral value of equality, how can you validly reason to a conclusion that says inter alia that equality is not intrinsically morally valuable at all?

Rawls in my judgment is innocent of the error that Cohen accuses him of making. Cohen himself starts with the strong antecedent opinion that equality of condition is a very important and central justice value, in fact for Cohen it turns out to be the entirety of distributive justice when properly elucidated. Holding this opinion, he finds it charitable to Rawls to impute to him similar views on the basis of his claims about the moral arbitrariness of the natural lottery. I admit these claims exhibit a Cheshire Cat elusiveness, but deny that they are best construed so as to reveal the argument Rawls builds from them to be incoherent.

However, not much hinges on this dispute. If it is true that Rawls moves from 'equality per se matters' premises to 'equality per se does not matter' conclusions, this merely indicates that Rawls, a pioneer in the articulation of contemporary egalitarianism, is not perfectly clear at the start about how the considerations that move him fit together into a plausible account of justice paired with good arguments supporting it. If Rawls ends up retracting some of what he asserts at the beginning of the discussion, that in itself is not a good reason to reject his final judgment that 'equality per se does not matter.'

The relevant passages in Rawls occur in chapters 1 and 2 of *A Theory of Justice*. In chapter one, explaining why the basic social structure deserves to be the primary subject of justice, Rawls states that over time the basic social structure brings it about that people begin their adult lives with very unequal holdings and prospects of primary social goods, and these initial inequalities cannot possibly be justified by appeal to individuals' differential desert. The fundamental task of a theory of distributive justice is to specify what justifies such inequalities when they are justified. In chapter two Rawls objects to the 'system of natural liberty,' roughly a society in which free speech and civil liberties are protected and a free market economy with private ownership of resources operates under the constraint of careers open to talents. Rawls observes:

> The existing distribution of income and wealth, say, is the cumulative effect of prior distributions of natural assets – that is, natural talents and abilities – as these have been developed or left unrealized, and their use favored or disfavored over time by social circumstances and such chance contingencies as accident and good fortune. Intuitively, the most obvious injustice of the system of natural liberty is that it permits distributive shares to be improperly influenced by these factors so arbitrary from a moral point of view.[12]

Rawls is appealing to a moral judgment he expects his readers to share, to the effect that when morally arbitrary factors such as sheer good and bad luck in people's initial social and natural circumstances and in the way that the ensemble of people's desires continually reshapes itself into supply and demand conditions significantly influence the outcomes of free market competitive trading over time, the mere fact that distributive outcomes result from free trading in a competitive market economy does not suffice to justify these outcomes. Something more is needed. In other words, all Rawls is committed to in the passage under examination is (a) there is some initial presumption in favor of

---

[12]   Rawls, *A Theory of Justice*, p. 63.

equal distribution and (b) the sheer fact that a distribution arises by free market trading, even by free market trading starting from a presumed fair starting point, does not suffice to overcome this initial presumption. Rawls says the system of natural liberty allows distributive shares to be 'improperly influenced' by the sheer luck of the natural lottery and market fluctuations. This suggests these factors might be regulated, without being eliminated or entirely offset, in such a way that they would properly influence distributive shares.

Rawls starts with a presumption in favor of equality of condition, and in the course of his reflections this presumption is overridden. In the end the presumption as it were disappears without trace. This need not betoken inconsistency. Analogy: One might start with a presumption in favor of the idea that when one is speaking to someone, one ought to be polite to that person. This presumption might be thought to be provisional. It disappears without a trace, for example, if one discovers one is addressing the person who brutally murdered your child and has shown no remorse. One might say the presumption is conditional: If the person one is speaking to has not done something that makes her the appropriate target of outraged or contemptuous or some other form of rude speech, there is a pro tanto moral reason to speak politely to that person.

A presumption in favor of equality of condition might be of any of a wide range of normative strengths. At one extreme, one might hold that if one knows nothing at all about a number of persons and one has to allocate goods among them somehow, since there is no basis for treating anyone asymmetrically, a respectful policy is to divide the goods equally across the persons. This very weak presumption gives way once any reason at all appears to give more goods to some rather than others. Alternatively, a presumption could be held to be stronger, and overrideable only by good enough reasons, and what counts as 'good enough' might be variously specified.

I don't mean to advance any heavy-duty theses that would substantially contribute to a moral theory of presumptions. My point is that a presumption can be provisional, in the sense that its presence at the start of inquiry is compatible with its entire disappearance without remainder by the end of inquiry, or compatible with its thoroughgoing transformation into a doctrine of a quite different character during the course of normative inquiry. And a presumption can vary in strength, down to the vanishing point.

Moral arbitrariness

Rawls exegesis aside, does the moral arbitrariness claim provide an argument for equality of condition?[13] Suppose one asks, would the fact that people's holdings came about via free and voluntary market trading from a fair initial starting point justify those present holdings? One might answer No on the ground that whatever moral principle required a certain pattern of holdings at the start, that same principle would almost certainly be violated as people's holdings change in the course of market interaction, so at some point a return to a distribution closer to the initial starting point would be required. (To argue in this way would be to run Robert Nozick's celebrated Wilt Chamberlain argument in reverse.[14]) In further support of that answer, one might add that the nature of free market trading is not such that it automatically provides legitimacy to whatever outcome results, especially after many rounds of trading. What one gets in trading depends on many chance circumstances including one's stock of traits and how those traits interact with the ensemble of supply and demand conditions to provide opportunities to some and deny opportunities to others.

The moral arbitrariness objection so construed objects to a proposed departure from an initial starting point. Nothing says this starting point has to be equality. One could just as well use the argument to defend feudal inequality, construed as presumptively normative. Suppose one begins with the natural inequality proposal: aristocrats should get more of the good things in life, because blue blood courses through their veins, and others should get less, because their blood is metaphysically inferior. The suggestion is then ventured that over time in free market trading, some non-aristocrats will end up with about as much as their natural superiors, and will deserve their holdings earned in market interaction, even though the end result is a trend toward equality of condition. Back comes the moral arbitrariness objection: It is sheer unmerited luck, good or bad, that renders some people able and others unable to command high prices for the goods and services they offer in market interaction. So the equalizing tendency of market interaction – its tendency not to

---

[13] On this question, see Susan Hurley, *Justice, Luck, and Knowledge* (Cambridge, MA: Harvard University Press, 2003).

[14] Robert Nozick, *Anarchy, State, and Utopia* (New York: Basic Books, 1974), pp. 160–164.

preserve the starting point inequality between the aristocrats and the others – is tainted by its source in a morally arbitrary causal process. The outcomes of market trading especially when repeated without redistributive correction over a long run, are determined in large part by accidents of birth, genetic endowment and favorable early socialization and education, and the like. Any equalization brought about by such a morally arbitrary process has no moral weight against the opposed norm of preserving an initially morally privileged starting point, in this case, feudal hierarchy and inequality by fixed rank.

The advocate of the moral arbitrariness argument construed as an argument for equality of condition might at this point be of the opinion that I have reinforced her case by this futile effort to tear it down. She now asserts that feudal hierarchy itself succumbs to the moral arbitrariness objection. Inequality of condition justified by the quality of individual lineage assessed by aristocratic standards is itself morally arbitrary if anything is. One finds oneself with aristocratic lineage or not as a sheer matter of brute luck beyond one's power to control. Seeing that one cannot use the moral arbitrariness objection to buttress any arbitrarily selected initial pattern of distribution suggests its inherent egalitarian affinity. Once one notices that choice or desert is the only morally nonarbitrary cause of unequal outcomes, one sees also straightaway that equality of condition is a morally privileged baseline – the two thoughts are flip sides of the same coin.

The easiest way to see that this train of thought is mistaken is to note that the moral arbitrariness objection in effect insists that what qualifies an individual as deserving or undeserving must not be a matter of sheer luck but must rather lie within her power to control. This idea can be embraced by someone who rejects equality of condition as any sort of distributive ideal – presumptive baseline, final end point, or anything in between. As I have already had occasion to mention, one might hold that it is bad – unjust and unfair – if some are worse off than others through no fault of their own and also hold it is bad – unjust and unfair – if some are just as well off as others through no merit of their own and interpret both assertions as partial statements of a moral meritocracy view: Each person should have good fortune or bad fortune over the course of her life in correspondence with what she deserves. Equality has no inherent value at all on this construal.

Moral arbitrariness again

Cohen finds in Rawls an argument from the moral arbitrariness of the sources of inequality to the claim that from the standpoint of distributive justice, it is unfair if some have less than others. This claim is qualified: It is unfair if some have less than others unless the inequality has a nonarbitrary cause. The argument according to Cohen does not begin with an assumed moral presumption in favor of equality of condition but rather establishes a moral presumption in favor of equality of condition.

I find this argument as Cohen presents it hard to construe, so I reproduce two of his formulations:

Cohen identifies his view as one that 'justifies equality as a starting point on the Rawlsian ground that the standard causes of inequality are morally arbitrary' (p. 155).

Page 156: 'the moral arbitrariness claim, which conjoins a post-medieval principle that none should be worse off than others through no fault of their own and modern sociological sophistication about the actual causes of how people fare' is said to 'put accidentally caused inequality under a cloud, as far as justice is concerned.'

The argument might be rendered as follows:

1. Differences in people's condition brought about by morally arbitrary causes are unjust.
2. The only causes of differences in people's condition that are not morally arbitrary involve differential desert.

Therefore

3. Differences in people's condition are unjust unless they are brought about by processes involving differential desert.

According to 3, inequalities that arise as incentive payments to specially talented individuals qualify as morally arbitrary and hence as unjust. Since only differential desert, or more broadly factors that lie within the individual's power to control, can generate inequality on a nonarbitrary basis, the Rawlsian attempt to begin with an argument from moral arbitrariness to a presumption in favor of equality and then to use that position as a foundation from which to establish the justice on inequalities that work to the advantage of the worst off is fundamentally flawed.

The moral arbitrariness argument establishes a tie between justice and equality that considerations of what is advantageous for this or that social group are unable to break.

The easiest way to see that the moral arbitrariness argument as construed by Cohen only supports a presumption of equality if it assumes this presumption at the outset is to note that the taint of moral arbitrariness can attach just as readily to equality as to inequality. Consider this argument:

1. Sameness in people's condition brought about by morally arbitrary causes is unjust.
2. The only causes of sameness in people's condition that are not morally arbitrary involve equal desert.

Therefore

4. Sameness in people's condition is unjust unless it is brought about by processes involving equality of desert.

Since what is sauce for the goose is sauce for the gander, the moral arbitrariness argument, if acceptable at all, is just as successful at establishing an apparent presumption in favor of inequality, in its second formulation, as it was in establishing an apparent presumption in favor of equality, in its first formulation. The operative word here is "apparent." In fact the two arguments are compatible; they involve an assertion of a moral meritocracy position: People ought to get gain better or worse conditions of life corresponding to their moral deservingness. The more deserving one is, the better one's condition ought to be. Distributive justice is distribution of good fortune corresponding to each individual's level of deservingness. Inequality of condition is unjust when it obtains among persons who are equally deserving and equality of condition is unjust when it obtains among persons who are unequally deserving.

The symmetrical position just described is broken only if one assumes at the outset that everyone's condition or quality of life ought to be the same, unless there is some special consideration in the circumstances that justifies inequality. This means that the argument that Cohen says establishes a presumption for equality in fact achieves that position only if one arbitrarily inserts the assumption of a presumption for inequality into the initial premise. No moral arbitrariness plus a presumption for equality implies a presumption for equality.

The moral arbitrariness argument as construed by Cohen is flawed in a more fundamental way than I have so far hinted at. The flaw lies in the idea of morally arbitrary causes of people's condition. Suppose that Mother Teresa has led an exemplary life, and Hitler has led a thoroughly evil life; the one is a saint and the other a villain. So far the circumstances of their lives have conspired to bring exactly the same degree of good fortune to each. Both are leading lives of middling quality. Then by chance a rock falls on one of the two; forever spoiling the injured person's life, because the injuries are painful, disabling, and can neither be healed nor offset by any available compensation. So inequality of condition then obtains: One of the two ends up leading a life that is good in the sense of good for the one who leads it (obtains the good that the virtue of prudence takes as its object). Surely any view of justice that allows a role to considerations of deservingness should hold that it issues in a more just outcome if it is Hitler and not Mother Teresa who is the one hit on the head by a rock with unfortunate consequences. However, if one holds with Cohen that it is morally bad (unjust and unfair) if some are worse off than others through no fault of their own, then one must hold that it is morally bad (unjust and unfair) that Hitler and Mother Teresa in this imaginary story end up unequally well off, with Hitler worse off – since in the story it is through sheer bad brute unchosen luck, and not any fault of his own that Hitler is bonked by the randomly falling rock with harmful consequences.

At this point the advocate of the moral arbitrariness argument might dig in her heels and defend the special causation requirement incorporated in it. One might deny that it is deservingness over the course of one's life – deservingness in the air, one might say – that determines one's eligibility for being on the short end or the long end of the stick when inequality might be established. Rather the justifiability of an inequality depends on how that particular inequality is brought about. Suppose that Emma voluntarily engages in a series of gambles, which might have turned out badly for her, but did not. Then she is hit by a random meteor. The risk of suffering this accident could not have been reduced or enhanced by any reasonable course of action she might have taken, and no meteor collision insurance was available to her. If Emma is now worse off than others through no choice of her own, this inequality is tainted by its morally arbitrary origin in sheer brute bad luck. The fact that she engaged in prior gambles that turned out to be inconsequential is neither here nor there for the assessment of the inequality of condition that now afflicts her.

The proposal under review now is that from the standpoint of distributive justice, it is unjust if some are worse off than others unless one who is worse off has freely chosen the course of action that led to this outcome (or could have, but did not, advert to a possible course of action one might have taken, that would have been reasonable to take and would likely have left her no worse off than others). The deservingness, merit, faultiness, or demerit of the agent's conduct is not relevant. I find this an unappealing construal of the Temkin luck egalitarian ideal, but let that pass. The proposal also seems to invoke an unspecified fair framework for interaction, within which choices that lead to your being worse off than others reduce your claims to restoration to equality, but let that pass. However, setting these issues aside, I still insist that this notion of moral arbitrariness works in tandem with the idea of a morally privileged baseline distribution, departures from which are then claimed to be acceptable only if nonarbitrary. The morally privileged baseline could be the distribution that is conducive to maximizing utility, or anything else. Nothing says it has to be equality.

Suppose we amend the moral arbitrariness argument in a way that eliminates the special causation requirement that had been built into it.

1. Differences in people's condition are unjust if they are brought about in such a way that there is no good justification for them.
2. The only good justification for differences in people's condition involves differential desert of the unequally placed individuals.

Therefore

3. Differences in people's condition are unjust unless they involve the differential desert of the unequally placed individuals.

The problem with the reformulated argument is that whereas premise 1 now is unexceptionable, premise 2 looks false. There are plausible justifiers of differences in people's condition, inequalities in their well-being or advantage levels enjoyed over the course of their lives, other than differential deservingness. One plausible candidate justifier is that the status quo could be improved by introducing an inequality that renders one or more persons better off and no one worse off. Another plausible candidate justifier is that the status quo could be improved by introducing an inequality that renders some better off and some worse off but in such a way that the gains of the gainers – discounted and amplified by the moral value of achieving gains for those persons given how well off or badly off they would otherwise be – exceeds the losses of the losers – discounted and amplified by the moral disvalue of imposing losses on those persons given how well off or badly off they would otherwise be. There are other plausible candidates.

Conclusion

There is much to like and embrace in *Rescuing Justice and Equality*. My arguments have focused on Cohen's attempt to rescue the idea of equality as a distributive justice ideal. Under examination, the attempt looks to be unsuccessful.

3

INEQUALITY, INJUSTICE AND LEVELLING DOWN

Thomas Christiano and Will Braynen

Abstract
The levelling down objection is the most serious objection to the
principle of equality, but we think it can be conclusively defeated.
It is serious because it pits the principle of equality squarely against
the welfares of the persons whose welfares or resources are equalized. It suggests that there is something perverse about the principle of equality. In this essay, we argue that levelling down is not an
implication of the principle of equality. To show this we offer a
defence of, and partial elaboration of, what we call a *common good
conception* of the principle of equality, which principle favours states
in which everyone is better off to those in which everyone is worse
off. We contrast this with what we call a *purely structural conception* of
the principle of equality. The common good conception of equality involves two basic components: (1) in each circumstance there
exists an ideal egalitarian distribution, which distributes equally
all the available good in the distribution with the highest average
welfare and (2) in evaluating how just the world is, it will matter
how far the actual distribution is from the ideal distribution. The
ideal egalitarian distribution in the circumstance is Pareto optimal
and the approximation rule implies that Pareto superior states are
less unjust than Pareto inferior states.[1]

Introduction

The levelling down objection is the most serious objection to the
principle of equality, but we think it can be conclusively defeated.
It is serious because it pits the principle of equality squarely
against the welfares of the persons whose welfares or resources
are equalized. It suggests that there is something perverse about
the principle of equality. Some of the usual examples of the
objection should give the flavour of this perversity. Probably the

---

[1]   We thank Geoffrey Brennan, David Chalmers, G. A. Cohen, John Deigh, Andrei
Marmor, Calvin Normore, Mark Schroeder, Andrew Williams, and Gideon Yaffe for helpful
discussion.

most notorious example is the lifeboat case in which there are, say, three people in a boat that is at risk of sinking unless one person is removed. All will die if no one is removed; only one will die if one person is removed. The common sense approach to this case is to distribute lots to each and select the person with the shortest (or longest) lot to be removed from the boat. But many argue that the principle of equality recommends that all die rather than that only one dies. The former outcome is egalitarian while the latter is inegalitarian. The claim is that the principle of equality favours levelling down the welfares of persons over the inequalities even though some are better off and no one is worse off under inequality. For another example, suppose two persons contribute in an equally deserving manner to the production of two goods. But the two goods cannot be divided and are of unequal worth. Some claim that the principle of equality would recommend throwing away the two goods in order that the two persons are not unequally rewarded. They say that equality may require levelling down rather than unequal rewards. For a final important example suppose that productive efficiency requires a significant use of markets and markets bring about inequalities that cannot be entirely effaced while a more centralized system of production is more equal in its rewards but far less productive. Some claim that the principle of equality implies that we ought to choose the centralized system of production even if everyone is better off under the partially decentralized system. Once again, the principle of equality is thought to imply the levelling down of the welfares of persons so as to ensure equality.

To be sure, those who embrace the idea that equality implies levelling down are careful to say that it is only one consideration among many. They may agree with most people that the one ought to die rather than all or that the goods ought to be distributed unequally. They simply say that the principle of equality implies levelling down but that there are other considerations that tell against levelling down, which often defeat the levelling down implication. Still, the idea is that the principle of equality itself implies levelling down.

Before continuing we want to point out that levelling down may apply for the same reasons to some non-egalitarian conceptions of distributive justice as they do to egalitarian ones. Consider comparative desert theories. Suppose that two people produce two things. One of these things is very valuable and the other is only a little bit and the things cannot be divided up. Now we must distribute these things between the two of them. Now suppose that one of them is a bit more deserving than the other but the two objects are very different in value so that their distribution cannot fit the differential merits. Indeed, the only way to fit the merits would be to give the small object to the more deserving person and destroy the large object. This is because the more deserving person is only a little more deserving and the smaller object has only a little value. Would such a desert theory require the destruction of the larger, more valuable object?

Here we can see pressures in the direction of distributing the more valuable object as well as pressures in the direction of destroying the more valuable object. On the one hand, some will say, the less deserving person deserves something. And if we distribute in accordance with the exact merits, the less deserving will not get anything. On the other hand, if we make sure the less deserving gets something, the less deserving will get much less than he deserves at least by comparison with the more deserving. Presumably similar reasoning could apply to principles that require distribution in accordance with need. So the worry about levelling down is much more general than an objection to equality.

One way to respond to the levelling down objection is to say that it is not an objection at all. This response accepts that equality does imply levelling down but that this is not a problem. Partly this response is predicated on the observation above that equality is only one consideration among many. We will argue in what follows that this is not a desirable way to go. We will show that there are considerations internal to the principle of equality (and many other comparative principles of justice) that suggest that if levelling down is a genuine implication of the principle of equality, then this is a real problem for the principle.

In this essay, we argue that levelling down is not an implication of the principle of equality. Indeed, we argue that the principle of equality, once properly understood, is opposed to levelling down. It always favours states in which everyone is better off, even if unequally so, to ones in which everyone is worse off even if equally well off. We will show that though the principle of equality implies that all inequalities are unjust, some inequalities are less unjust than some equalities, namely those in which everyone is worse off. To the extent that the levelling down objection is the principal objection to the principle of equality, we think this argument should go a long way to undermining opposition to the principle of equality.

To show this we offer a defence of, and partial elaboration of, what we call a *common good conception* of the principle of equality, which principle favours states in which everyone is better off to those in which everyone is worse off. We contrast this with what we call a *purely structural conception* of the principle of equality. The purely structural conception of equality evaluates distributions of goods exclusively in terms of the comparisons across persons. On this conception the only information relevant, from the point of view of the principle of equality, to the evaluation of distributions of goods are comparisons across persons in terms of their welfare or opportunities for welfare. A purely structural conception of equality does imply levelling down and if the arguments of this essay are sound this is reason to prefer the common good conception over the purely structural conception.

To give a brief preview, the common good conception of equality will involve two basic components: (1) in each circumstance there exists an ideal distribution (or the ideally just distribution), and (2) in evaluating how just the world is, it will matter how far your actual distribution is from the ideal distribution. Thus, the first step is to identify the ideally just distribution. On our theory, this ideal distribution is an equal distribution of the feasible goods available in the circumstances. We note that the general strategy we outline in this essay should be of interest to any distributive justice theorist who is concerned with the justice of patterns.[2] A comparative desert theorist for example, might instead argue that the ideally just distribution is something else. The second step is to use one's ideal theory (the ideal distribution) to evaluate any actual or current state of affairs (some arbitrary distribution) by measuring the difference from the ideal distribution to the actual distribution. In other words, to know exactly how unjust some arbitrary distribution is, we want to know by how much that distribution diverges from the ideally just distribution. It is in these two steps that the levelling down objection is defeated. The ideal distribution equalizes all the feasible gains in a circumstance and thus does not waste any goods. The rule of approximation then says that while inequalities are unjust, they

---

[2]   Not all distributive theories are of this sort of course. Nozick's libertarian theory of property entitlement that is governed by a just process denies that patterns or distributions occupy a central place in a theory of distributive justice because on Nozick's view, a just process will upset any distribution of goods. See *Anarchy, State and Utopia* (New York: Basic Books, 1974), chapter 7.

are not as unjust as equalities in which everyone is worse off. It is this idea that we defend and elaborate in this essay.[3]

In what follows we present a version of the levelling down objection using cardinal and interpersonally comparable utilities. We then give an argument for why egalitarians (and by implication many other comparative principles of distributive justice) should take the levelling down objection seriously. Then we show that there is a fundamental gap in the argument that alleges that levelling down is an implication of equality. Finally we elaborate and defend a conception of equality that rejects levelling down. And we elaborate a rule for comparing distributions of goods.

The levelling down objection

It has been said by some that the principle of egalitarian justice is subject to a fatal intuitive objection. The objection is that the principle of equality has an extremely implausible implication. Suppose two alternative states $(2, 2)$ and $(7, 3)$ in which two persons are represented in terms of the amount of welfare they each enjoy in that state. The numbers are cardinal and represent interpersonally comparable utilities. To some, the principle of equality appears to say that $(7, 3)$ is worse than $(2, 2)$ at least in the respect relevant to the principle of equality. This is because $(2, 2)$ is egalitarian while $(7, 3)$ is not. $(7, 3)$ represents a departure from equality while $(2, 2)$ does not. Thus the principle of equality appears to imply that, at least as far as equality is concerned, we ought to make everyone worse off. Of course, other principles may contend with equality and override its recommendation in this case. But the worry is that to the extent that the principle of egalitarian justice makes the recommendation that everyone be made worse off, that is a strike against the principle.[4]

---

[3] A positive argument for the principle of equality understood according to the common good conception is in Thomas Christiano, 'A Foundation for Equality', *Egalitarianism: New Essays on The Nature and Value of Equality*, ed. Nils Holtug and Kasper Lippert-Rasmussen (Oxford: Oxford University Press, 2007) and in Chapter 1 of Thomas Christiano, *The Constitution of Equality: Democratic Authority and Its Limits* (Oxford: Oxford University Press, 2008).

[4] See Derek Parfit, 'Equality or Priority?', The Lindley Lecture (University of Kansas, 1991), p. 23 for an account of the objection. See also Jan Narveson, 'On Dworkinian Equality', *Social Philosophy and Policy*, Volume 1, issue 1, pp. 1–22, Harry Frankfurt, 'Equality

Why the levelling down objection matters

The levelling down objection would be a real problem for the principle of equality, were it true that levelling down was an implication of the principle of equality.[5] For most egalitarians seem to hold both to the idea that equality is important and to the idea that well-being is important (or at least opportunity for or access to well-being or capacities for functioning). And these two judgments seem to come together in their egalitarianisms. For one thing, many egalitarians think that the promotion of well-being or at least the opportunities or access to well-being is important.[6] This suggests that these egalitarians cannot be indifferent between two egalitarian states (2, 2) and (5, 5), which are such that everyone is better off in the latter. Egalitarians must prefer the Pareto superior equality to the Pareto inferior equality, and that preference derives from the correct understanding of the principle of equality, or so we will argue.

Here is the basic argument for this thesis. In what follows we will usually speak for simplicity's sake as if well-being is the relevant metric for equality. We think the same considerations will hold for any other fundamental good that serves as a metric of equality such as resources (as Dworkin defines them) or opportunities for welfare or access to advantage. There is an internal connection between the rationale for equality and the value of the relevant fundamental good that is equalized. If it were not true that more well-being is better than less, then there would be no point to equality. There would be no reason to care about equality. Since the importance of well-being seems to be built in to the rationale for the principle of equality – it is the reason for the principle taking the shape that it does – an egalitarian cannot be indifferent between these two states.

as a Moral Ideal', in his *The Importance of What We Care About* (Cambridge: Cambridge University Press, 1998), for other sympathetic accounts of this objection.

 [5]   Not everyone agrees that this is a strike against the principle of egalitarian justice. Larry Temkin argues that there are other principles that may have strongly Pareto inefficient implications. Temkin cites principles of retributive desert that imply in some circumstances that everyone ought to be worse off than they could because they deserve to be worse off. He argues that many accept such a view despite its welfare diminishing character. See Larry Temkin, 'Equality, Priority and the Leveling Down Objection', in *The Ideal of Equality*, ed. Mathew Clayton and Andrew Williams (New York: St. Martin's Press, 2000), pp. 126–161, esp. p. 138.

 [6]   See G. A. Cohen, 'The Currency of Egalitarian Justice', *Ethics*, October 1989 for a thorough discussion of some different options for understanding the metric of equality.

To take an example, suppose that we are concerned with distributing bread among persons and we have much more than is needed. In this context there is a definite level at which each person has enough and beyond which more does not matter. In this context we would only be concerned that each receive enough of the bread and beyond that we would not care how much each gets. Beyond the satisfaction of need and culinary taste whether we distribute equal amounts of bread or not would be, in and of itself, a matter of indifference.[7]

To be sure, if we did not have enough for everyone, we might be concerned with equal distribution. So if we had enough for everyone to survive but not enough to satisfy everyone we would be concerned with the correct distribution of bread. But in this case, it is precisely because the amount of bread we have is such that more is better than less for everyone that we concern ourselves with its distribution.

Another example is a concern over how many letters people have in their last names. For the most part people are indifferent to how many letters they have in their names. As a consequence, they will be indifferent to the quantitative distribution of letters in each person's name. Equality could not be important in this context.

So a necessary condition for equality mattering is that the thing being equalized is such that more is better than less. We want to argue that since the truth of the proposition that more substantial good is better than less substantial good is a necessary condition for there being a rationale for the principle of equality in the substantial good, the right account of the principle of equality must somehow include the idea that equalities in which everyone is better off are better than equalities in which everyone is worse off.

Clearly this proposition is not a conceptual one. One can imagine a principle of equality of shares in substantial good that does not concern itself with whether people have more of that substantial good. But the question is: does such a principle make

---

[7] To be sure, if each person could sell his excess bread, then equality above the level of enough bread would make sense. The observation about the distribution of bread not mattering above the level of sufficiency is the central insight of defenders of sufficiency theories such as Harry Frankfurt in his 'Equality as a Moral Ideal'. For critiques of sufficiency as a general account of distributive justice see Paula Casal, 'Why Sufficiency Is Not Enough', *Ethics*, 117 (January 2007), pp. 296–326 and Thomas Christiano, 'A Foundation for Egalitarianism'.

sense? The things of which we care about egalitarian distribution are things that we want more of rather than less for everyone. And it is because we want more of rather than less of these things for everyone that we think that egalitarian distribution of these things matters.

Moreover, the values over which the principle of equality ranges do not have any components that justify lowering the welfares of persons (or the opportunity for welfare). To appreciate this, note the contrast with some other conceptions of justice. Suppose one holds a non-comparative desert principle that states that the vicious ought to suffer and the virtuous ought to thrive. If every person in a society is vicious, then they all deserve to be badly off. This would favour a Pareto inefficient outcome in which everyone is badly off. The introduction of a new set of resources that could make everyone better off would not be an improvement; indeed, on the desert theory if everyone were to be made better off than they deserved to be, that would be worse. On these views, it is better that a person who deserves it be worse off. This is part of the value theory of these conceptions of desert. We may reject this value theory, but it makes some sense and levelling down makes sense in the context of this kind of principle. But there is no analogous feature in egalitarian principles. The egalitarian theorists are not in the position of the non-comparative desert theorist. There is nothing in the value theory that says that it is better for a person to be worse off.

Because there is an internal connection between the importance of equality and the idea that it is better to have more rather than less of the thing being equalized, the levelling down objection is an objection that ought to be taken seriously by egalitarians, if it works. But we do not think that it works. That is we do not think that levelling down is an implication of the principle of equality. And the fact that it does not work can be seen in a number of ways.

A gap in the levelling down objection

The levelling down objection derives its apparent strength from the claim that an egalitarian must think that something is lost when there is some inequality. This claim follows from the central egalitarian claim that all inequalities are unjust. And from this it is inferred that any egalitarian distribution must be better than any non-egalitarian distribution, at least in one respect. And from this it is inferred that there is one important respect in which an egalitarian distribution is better than a Pareto superior state (i.e. a state in which at least one person is better off and no one is worse off).

But, the inference above is problematic. From the observation that there is loss from inequality it does not follow that every egalitarian distribution is better in respect of the principle of equality than every non-egalitarian distribution. What the egalitarian must say is that every non-egalitarian distribution is unjust because it is not equal. Only equality is fully just. But the egalitarian need not say that every egalitarian state is better than every non-egalitarian state.

How can it be that only equality is just but not that every equality is better than every inequality? The basic idea is that the egalitarian can and should say that for every circumstance, there is an ideal egalitarian distribution such that failure to realize that ideal egalitarian distribution in the circumstances is unjust. Instead of identifying a purely structural feature of distributions that can be satisfied just as much by Pareto inferior states as by Pareto superior states, the present suggestion is that the principle of equality identifies first and foremost an ideal distribution in each relevant circumstance. It is this ideal distribution that embodies what is fully just in the circumstance. Any departure from this ideal distribution in the circumstance is unjust. A complete principle of equality then defines a rule of approximation to this ideal egalitarian distribution. It determines which departures from the ideal egalitarian distribution are more unjust and which are less unjust. It gives a ranking of states in terms of how close to the ideal egalitarian distribution they are. Our thought is that this rule of approximation need not entail that all equalities, no matter how inefficient, are better than all inequalities. This is a substantive matter on which there must be argument for one rule over another.

To see this, think of the division of a pie between two equally deserving people and where nothing else is to be taken into account, so this is a complete description of the circumstances of justice for these two people. The ideal egalitarian distribution of this pie is to cut it in two pieces of equal size. That is what egalitarian justice requires in the circumstance. Any other division is, let us suppose, unjust. Now ask how other divisions of this pie would rank in terms of closeness to the ideal distribution.

Suppose, for some crazy reason, that the pie could not be cut into equal parts. It can only be cut into two somewhat unequal parts or the whole thing could be thrown away. The question for the principle of equality as we understand it here is which of these two alternative distributions is less unjust? And the way to answer this question is to determine which of the two alternative distributions is closest in terms of justice to the ideal egalitarian distribution. Once the egalitarian has identified the ideal egalitarian distribution and has asserted that all other distributions are unjust in the circumstance, there is no reason to suppose that the egalitarian must think that the distribution closest in justice to the ideal distribution is the one in which the pie is thrown away. It is a nontrivial task to determine what rule of approximation to use in deciding which distribution is closest to the ideal distribution. We may think that a rule of approximation to the ideal that ranks the Pareto superior but unequal division as less unjust than the Pareto inferior but equal division is the best one. Indeed we will vindicate this thesis in what follows. But for now it is worth noting that holding to a principle of equality does not require that one choose the approximation rule that favours the Pareto inferior equality. Hence, levelling down need not be an implication of a principle of equality.

Consider the three states we have discussed so far in abstract terms. (2, 2) and (5, 5) are egalitarian and (7, 3) is non-egalitarian. (5, 5) and (7, 3) are both strongly Pareto superior to (2, 2). (7, 3) and (5, 5) are Pareto non-comparable.[8] But (5, 5) is egalitarian and (7, 3) is not. The difference is that in (7, 3) at least one person is better off and another is worse off than in (5, 5). All the egalitarian is committed to asserting is that there is something lost in (7, 3) because all the people are not equally well off. This may merely imply that (5, 5) is better or more just than (7, 3). It is compatible with this to say that (7, 3) is better or more just than (2, 2), just as (5, 5) is. And this set of claims is sufficient to make sense of the claim that for every inequality, there is something lost with respect to equality.

Of course, (5, 5) may not be feasible but this need not be a reason to think that it is not what justice requires in the circumstance or that (7, 3) is defective precisely because it diverges from

---

[8]   Two states are 'Pareto non-comparable' when they have different distributions but neither is Pareto superior to the other.

(5, 5). As we see it, a state of affairs can be unjust even if there is no way to improve it and we can have a conception of what is just under the circumstances even if we cannot bring about that justice. Justice does not obey the 'ought implies can' principle entirely. In part, it serves as an ideal to be approximated.

We can see this in a variety of contexts. We know that even the best penal system is likely to convict some innocent persons and let some guilty persons go free and we are inclined to think that these are injustices even though we cannot improve the system that makes these errors beyond a certain point. We think we can see it in a distributive case as well. If two persons have contributed equally to the production of a pair of unequal but indivisible substantial goods, we may think that there is some injustice in giving the better good to one and the lesser good to the other. Each person in the circumstance will feel some regret at the imperfect justice of the distribution, even if they use a lottery to determine who gets what. No one can be blamed for the inequality and the use of an egalitarian lottery goes some way to alleviating the sense of injustice but it does not go away entirely.

All that is needed for the egalitarian is to say that the unequal state is missing something or is unjust because it is not equal. This is still an importantly egalitarian theory but it does not say that any equality is better in some respect than any inequality. It says there is an ideal egalitarian distribution in each circumstance and that every inequality is unjust because it is not equal.

What our argument so far has shown is that there is a significant gap in the levelling down objection against equality. It has shown that a crucial inference is unsupported by the objector and that alternatives to that inference are logically possible. What we want to show in the next section is that the logically possible alternative missed by the proponents of the levelling down objection is in fact the best account of equality.

What we argue for in the following is not a complete principle but a strategy for constructing such a principle. We do not have the time to construct a complete principle and we are not sure we can do it at the moment anyway. But it is a defensible strategy, which implies that there is some principle that satisfies the strategy, which is the correct principle of equality. If this is a legitimate strategy, then it is sufficient to defeat the levelling down objection.

An argument for Pareto optimal inequalities

There are a number of cases in which inequality is Pareto superior to feasible equality. In one sort of case, some goods are lumpy, so we cannot achieve a completely egalitarian distribution. The second case involves production. In some cases, the complexities and uncertainties of production require that incentives be offered to those who are most suited to the tasks to be performed. In this kind of case, inequalities arise as a kind of by product of the process of production.[9] A third case is the lifeboat case in which it is not possible that every person live equally good lives. Our thesis is that if all persons can be made better off than under the best feasible equality, then the principle of equality we have defended implies that we should choose that state in which some are better off and none are worse off than under the best feasible equality.

First, we will consider whether it is just to bring about a strong Pareto improvement over feasible equality. So we will compare just two states and we will just consider this for two persons: A and B. This is a narrow idealization but it is hard enough to grasp it properly. The argument proceeds by comparing two states: (2, 2) in which A and B are equally well off and (7, 3) in which both are better off than in the first but A is better off than B.

The strong Pareto improvement in (7, 3) pushes us in a direction that does not allow us fully to satisfy the constraint stated by the principle of equality. There is a failure of justice in cases of unequal distribution. In our example, either A is being treated better than the reasons allow in his case or B is being treated worse than the reasons allow in his case or both of these claims are true.

If we compare (2, 2) (feasible equality) and (7, 3) (feasible strong Pareto improvement) the egalitarian principle of justice says that there is something wrong in (7, 3) because it is not equal.

---

[9]   G. A. Cohen has argued quite persuasively in his *Rescuing Justice and Equality* (Cambridge, Mass.: Harvard University Press, 2008), chapter 1, that there is something problematic from the standpoint of justice in allowing more talented persons to receive more as an incentive to work than others receive. This argument casts serious doubt on Rawls's use of incentives in this context in *A Theory of Justice* (Cambridge, MA: Harvard University Press, 1971). But incentives may still be required for informational purposes and it may be impossible to wipe the inequalities entirely away without significant cost. See Christiano's 'Cohen on Incentives and Inequality', in *Ethics and Economics*, ed. Christi Favor, Gerald Gaus and Julian Lamont (Palo Alto, CA: Stanford University Press, 2009) for this argument.

But we want to say that there is something even worse in (2, 2) with regard to justice. And so we have reason to prefer the feasible strong Pareto improvement to the feasible equality, from the point of view of justice. What is our reason for this?

The reason is grounded in a common good conception of equality or a conception of equality that includes a concern to advance the interests of each and every person. This conception is the basis of a plausible strategy for constructing a principle of equality that gives us a plausible account of greater and smaller departures from equality. Both (2, 2) and (7, 3) may be unjust and thus departures from justice, but the question is, which one is a greater departure from justice? We will propose a strategy for constructing a principle that gives us a schematic account of how to assess the size of the departure from ideal equality.

The strategy for constructing the principle comes in two stages: first the strategy calls for a rule identifying the ideal egalitarian distribution in a given circumstance. Second, the strategy calls for a rule for assessing greater and lesser departures from the ideal egalitarian distribution.

The ideal egalitarian distribution

The first step is to identify that distribution that would be ideally just in the circumstances. On an egalitarian theory that would be an egalitarian distribution of the substantial goods involved in the circumstances. And this is the distribution relative to which all states are evaluated in the circumstances by justice. Our proposal is that the ideal egalitarian distribution in a given circumstance is a potential Pareto optimal distribution. That distribution is better for the worst off person in the feasible Pareto optimal inequality but not as good for the better off person in the feasible inequality. Since the ideal egalitarian distribution may not be feasible, it is only a potential Pareto optimal point. In the abstract numerical example we are discussing, the ideal egalitarian distribution is (5, 5) in which B is better off than in (7, 3) but A is worse off. And A and B are better off than in the feasible egalitarian state.

How do we determine the ideal egalitarian distribution in a particular situation? First, we need to say how we identify a circumstance. We propose to identify a circumstance or situation in terms of the highest level of average utility that is feasible for the persons involved. So in the numerical example the state that gives the highest feasible level of average utility of 5 per person is (7, 3) by hypothesis. The circumstance for which we are trying to define the ideal egalitarian distribution is identified by this highest available average utility. If we find that more average utility is possible than previously because of increased production or more manna from heaven then we have moved to a new circumstance.

Second, in order to define the ideal egalitarian distribution for the circumstance we propose to take the highest average level of well-being between A and B in the circumstance and say that the ideal distribution consists in each getting that level of well-being. So for a circumstance in which (7, 3) has the highest feasible average utility, (5, 5) is the ideal egalitarian distribution. To be sure, sometimes this ideal egalitarian distribution is not feasible and sometimes it is.

Combining these two elements, the numerical example we have given tells us that (5, 5) is the ideal egalitarian distribution in the circumstance. Should the circumstances change and a higher average become available, then the ideal egalitarian distribution would change as well. The thought is that there is an ideal egalitarian distribution for every circumstance. To be sure, in most circumstances, there are a number of possible Pareto optimal states. The above rule says that the ideal egalitarian distribution in a particular situation is the mean level of well-being of the best (understood in terms of the total well-being) feasible Pareto optimal state.

A number of considerations favour this way of identifying the ideal egalitarian distribution. One, this conception of the ideal egalitarian distribution accommodates the idea that there is an internal connection between the rationale for the principle of equality and the importance to each person of the thing being equalized. It does this in two ways. First, it does this by using the device of an ideal distribution against which all other distributions in a circumstance are to be evaluated as opposed to evaluating distributions merely on the basis of their structural features. The use of the ideal distribution implies that there is a certain level of provision of goods that is important to justice in a circumstance. A purely structural approach to equality, in contrast, states that all that matters to egalitarians is the shape of the distribution. Such an approach seems to ignore altogether the value of the things being distributed. Second, the ideal egalitarian distribution implies that each should have the highest average level of good that is available.

Two, it seems like a natural egalitarian distribution for the circumstance because it equalizes all the gains from the best feasible Pareto optimal state available. And it seems that this is a natural interpretation of the grounds of regret people might have when two equally deserving people produce two unequally valued and indivisible objects. In our pie example, supposing for some strange reason that it cannot be cut equally, the two equally deserving contributors to the making of the pie will not want to throw it away but they may still experience some regret at the fact that the pie is not distributed equally.

In the lifeboat example we have discussed, in which one person out of the five must be tossed out in order to preserve anyone at all, the ideal egalitarian distribution might involve an equal distribution of the total number of years to live available to the group. In this case, supposing that the remaining four expect to live another thirty years each, the ideal egalitarian distribution would be that all five live twenty four years each. When one person is thrown out of the boat, each has reason to regret that the burden falls entirely on that one person even if the choice of person is made by lot. A natural way to interpret this regret is that the burden did not fall equally on each in such a way that each could have an equal life span. Presumably if this option had been available, they would have chosen this were they egalitarians. They seem to be regretting what has happened because they are evaluating it against a standard of ideal egalitarian distribution.

Three, this conception of the ideal egalitarian distribution seems to strike the right balance between considerations of realism and the ideal in thinking about principles of justice. We have defended the ideal egalitarian distribution against the charge that it is sometimes infeasible. Feasibility is not a necessary condition for justice and the infeasibility of better alternatives is not a sufficient basis for saying that there is nothing wrong with the feasible state. We can see this in the cases of necessarily imperfect penal systems, and with the kinds of regrets we experience when a fully just distribution is not feasible. At the same time, though, this conception of the ideal egalitarian distribution represents a kind of ideal that is suited to the circumstances at hand. The circumstances are defined by the available amount of good to the group in question and in terms of the best feasible Pareto optimal state. Though the ideal equality may not itself be achievable in the circumstances it is nevertheless connected in a realistic way to the circumstances.

So the ideal egalitarian distribution is not merely pie in the sky. Indeed it has real bite. This is because it says that the best off in the Pareto optimal inequalities are unjustly advantaged and the worst off are unjustly disadvantaged.[10] We will also see that it has bite to it when we elaborate a plausible rule for approximating to the ideal egalitarian distribution.

Approximations to justice

The second stage is grounded in the idea that when ideal justice is not achievable, we may still have a conception of what is closer to the ideal and what is further away. In particular, we may still have a conception of what is more just and what is less just in relation to the ideal. And for this we develop a rule for determining approximations to justice. An egalitarian theory will determine which departures from the ideal egalitarian distribution are greater departures from justice and which departures are smaller ones. The smaller departures from justice are more just or less unjust than the greater departures from justice. In this way, even if the ideal egalitarian distribution is not feasible itself, it sets an ideal to which we can approximate and the principles governing the measurement of approximation are what we are concerned with in this second stage. In this way, the ideal egalitarian distribution has practical significance even if it cannot be realized.

We will canvass a couple of proposals in this essay to give a sense of how to think this problem through before we provide what seems to us to be an acceptable rule. First we will discuss what we call the difference summing method of measuring approximations to justice. Then we will propose a more complex method of assessing approximations that is meant to resolve the difficulties in the first approach.

---

[10] One way that we would argue we should not specify the ideal egalitarian distribution is to say that the equality at the highest level of well-being is the only fully just arrangement. The reason for this rejection is that such a principle would not be distinctively egalitarian. This is because it would say what non-egalitarians could readily agree to, which is that Pareto improvements are to be pursued. We doubt if many want to disagree with that. What makes the principle of equality distinctive is that it recommends making some people worse off if that will make others better off and it recommends this up to the point of equality.

Criteria for a good rule

First, we will describe what we take to be some plausible constraints on the construction of such a rule. These constraints mostly are implied by the ideas underlying the principle of equality.

The first and clearest constraint on the construction of such a rule is that the most just state of affairs in the circumstances must be the ideal egalitarian distribution. So the rule will recommend the ideal equality whenever it is feasible. Because this is an egalitarian theory, we assume that the ideally just distribution in any given circumstance is egalitarian (but not that any egalitarian distribution is ideal or even desirable since, as we have argued above, such a distribution could be very far from the ideal).

The second constraint on the approximation rule is that the rule must never favour Pareto inferior states over Pareto superior states. This aspect of the rule follows from the importance of the well-being of all persons that is essential to the principle of equality. And this aspect of the rule is what ensures that the principle of equality never implies levelling down.

The third constraint on the rule of approximation is that the rule does not track average or total utility because it is not a utilitarian rule. There will be cases in which some states are closer approximations to the ideal egalitarian distribution than others even though the others have a greater amount of average utility. This aspect of the rule of approximation follows from the fact that the principle at issue is not a utilitarian principle and so will prefer many egalitarian states that have lower average utility. But remember this condition is to be combined with the second condition that says that the rule never selects Pareto inferior states as more just than Pareto superior states. Thus the rule will select some states that have less average utility than others on condition that they are all Pareto non-comparable.

The fourth and final constraint on the rule of approximation tells us that the rule must not depart too much from the difference principle. This does not follow directly from any of the aspects of the principle of equality that we have defended. It is an intuitive idea about approximating equality. But it requires some explanation. One, we say that the rule must not depart too far from the difference principle because we think that some realizations of the difference principle get very close to levelling down and are what we call quasi-levelling down. For example if we imagine two states of affairs such that in one each is equally well off and in the other one person is much better off while another is only a tiny bit worse off than in the equal state, the difference principle will favour the equal distribution. And we can make it so that the difference between the worst off person in the unequal state of affairs and those in the equal state of affairs is arbitrarily small though still significant. The difference principle will always prefer the equal state even if the advantage to the worst off is extremely small while the advantage to the better in the unequal state is much greater. This seems to us to suggest that the difference principle involves something like levelling down in some circumstances, what we call quasi-levelling down. Still, the difference principle in many circumstances does seem to give an intuitively plausible answer to the question of what the best approximation to ideal equality is and so we say that the approximation rule should not be the same as the difference principle but it should not depart too far from it. Admittedly, this is a vague constraint, but our intention here is just to give a sense of what a rule of approximation to ideal equality is that does not imply levelling down. It is worthwhile noting here that this explains two features of the difference principle. One, it is not a principle of justice in the sense that it defines ideal justice in a circumstance. Hence, this approach departs from Rawls's conception of the difference principle as a principle of justice. Nevertheless, the difference principle does stand out in many circumstances as the best way to approximate full justice and so it can be thought of as a principle of justified injustice or even as a principle of the least unjust outcome (with the caveat noted above that it does not always pick out the least unjust state).

The difference summing rule of approximation

Our initial proposal is to measure the departures from justice in terms of the sum of differences in well-being between the state being evaluated and the ideal egalitarian distribution. And the state in which the sum of differences from the ideal egalitarian distribution is smallest is closer to ideal equality and so is the more just state. More formally, this principle is given by the following function: $d(S_{actual}, S_{ideal}) = |x^* - x| + |y^* - y|$ between the ideal distribution (x^*, y^*) and the actual distribution (x, y). The hope is that d will be closer to zero as the actual distribution gets closer to the ideal distribution. This too seems like a natural method, but as we will see, it will require some modification. Let us call this the *difference summing principle.*

For (7, 3) we add the difference in well-being for person B between (7, 3) and (5, 5) to the difference in well-being for person A between (7, 3) and (5, 5). And for (2, 2) we add the difference in well-being for B between (2, 2) and (5, 5) to the difference in well-being for A between (2, 2) and (5, 5). If the sum of differences is greater for (2, 2) than for (7, 3), then (2, 2) is a greater departure from justice than (7, 3). And we can see that this holds in this case. There the sum of differences between (2, 2) and (5, 5) is 6. While the sum of differences between (7, 3) and (5, 5) is 4. In general, for the two person cases, this will imply that feasible strong Pareto improvements will be more just than the Pareto inferior feasible equality. This is because the two persons' welfares in the strong Pareto improvement are closer to their welfares in the ideal equality than are the welfares in the Pareto inferior feasible equality. Therefore, the principle of equality that accords with this strategy will say that the strong Pareto improvements are superior to the Pareto inferior feasible equality. To be sure both are unjust, but one is more unjust than the other.

The strategy accords with the kind of principle of equality that values both well-being and a non-arbitrary way in which it is distributed because the ideal egalitarian distribution is the product of a concern for well-being and a non-arbitrary distribution. The requirement of non-arbitrariness ensures that the ideal distribution is one of equality; the concern for well-being ensures that the Pareto superior inequality is more just than the Pareto inferior equality. And the method of assessing departures from equality in terms of the sum of differences of well-being from the ideal equality point seems a highly intuitive way of capturing all these concerns and the idea of departures from equality.

Furthermore, note that the difference summing rule does not give exclusive priority to well-being. Some states that are egalitarian will be superior to some states that are unequal even if the unequal state has more average utility. You can see this in the following numerical example. Here (5, 5) is the ideal egalitarian distribution. (7, 3) has the same average utility as (5, 5) and (4, 4) has a lower average utility than the ideal or (7, 3). Nevertheless, by the difference summing rule, (4, 4) is more just than (7, 3).

This seems like a good result to us. First, the equality that is Pareto inferior to the ideal equality is unjust. It is, however, less unjust than the best Pareto non-comparable inequality. And, second, the equality that is Pareto inferior to the inequality is less just than the inequality.

It makes sense that a principle of equality would have the implication of sometimes choosing a state in which the total amount of well-being is not maximized because the principle of equality does not track the principle of average utility and the principle of approximation does not track it either. So the thought is that equality can be more just than inequality even if the inequality includes more total utility. This is a welcome result if, like us, you want to reject utilitarianism and so do not want to simply track total or average utility.

But there are serious difficulties with the difference summing rule. To see these, suppose that we have three states (10, 0), (5, 5) and (1, 1). (10, 0) is the best feasible Pareto Optimal state for person A and person B because it has the highest average well-being. (5, 5) is the ideal egalitarian distribution but is not feasible. (1, 1) is an egalitarian point that is inferior to (5, 5) but it is non-comparable to (10, 0). So the situation is as described above so far. The sum of differences of (1, 1) from (5, 5) is 8. The sum of differences of (10, 0) from (5, 5) is 10. So here it looks like (1, 1) is more just than (10, 0). Maybe one isn't disturbed by this implication but this experiment can be repeated to the point where the worst off of the equality is only slightly better off than the worst off in the Pareto optimal inequality. This would be the case if in the feasible equality A and B both had 0.1 as in (0.1, 0.1). Yet it is more just than (10, 0). And we can of course push this further to say (0.0001, 0.0001). It is still better than (10, 0). We are getting asymptotically close to a levelling down objection. No matter how small the difference is between the worst off in the equality from that in the Pareto optimal inequality, the equality is superior. This seems like a very troubling result. Let us call this the *quasi levelling down objection* to the difference summing proposal.

But there is another levelling down objection to the difference summing proposal in the near vicinity. Suppose we take (10, 0) again as the best feasible Pareto optimal inequality and we take (5, 5) as the ideal equality. Now suppose we find that there is a state (5, 0) in which the worst off is the same as the worst off in (10, 0) but the better off is at or near (5, 5) or only slightly better off. So (5, 0) is Pareto inferior to (10, 0) but the sum of differences between (10, 0) and (5, 5) is greater than the sum of differences between (5, 0) and (5, 5). Here the rule minimizing the sum of differences from ideal equality seems to say (5, 0) is better than (10, 0) even though it is Pareto inferior. And note that the rule implies that the Pareto inferior distribution is better than the Pareto superior one all the way to the point in which the better off person in the Pareto inferior distribution is only slightly better off than the worst off person. Hence (0.1, 0) is, on the difference summing rule, superior to (10, 0). The difference summing rule of approximation seems to rank some Pareto inferior states above some Pareto superior states, which violates our concern with well-being. These are cases of weakly Pareto inferior distributions being preferred to weakly Pareto superior distributions (in which some persons are better off and no one is worse off). And we think that the concern for well-being implicit in the principle of equality should imply that the weakly Pareto superior distribution should be preferred. Furthermore, we can see that the difference summing rule will also prefer some strongly Pareto inferior distributions to the strongly superior. Just consider the example of (9, 1) and (5, 0). Here the sums of the differences from ideal equality amount to 8 and 5 respectively. These are instances of what we call the *nested levelling down objection.*

These two levelling down worries seem to us to show that we need another principle of approximation to equality if we are to have a satisfactory conception of equality.

The divergence rule of approximation

We think it is intuitively clear that we can construct a rule that satisfies the four constraints stated above and thereby avoids the worries that apply to the difference summing rule. In this section we will construct such a rule.

This problem of having a rule for comparing an actual distribution to an ideal distribution is in fact formally similar to a class of problems outside political philosophy. One example is evaluating how good a given scientific theory is. Perhaps the most famous way to pick between competing theories is Occam's razor. This, however, is not the only way. Another way to evaluate how well a given theory describes the data is to see how close it gets to the data. The data (or observations) is represented as a probability distribution. So is a theory. The theory is then thought of as an arbitrary distribution (because we can have more than one theory describing the same set of data), whereas the data is thought as the unique ideal distribution. Whichever theory (as a probability distribution) diverges less from the observed data (also represented as a probability distribution) better describes the data. This can be thought of as information divergence or relative entropy. The same technique seems appropriate in the case of ideal political theory when one deals with distributions. Instead of probability distributions, however, a welfare egalitarian will have to evaluate and compare welfare distributions (i.e. distributions of well-being across persons).[11]

For contrast, consider the utilitarian measure of evaluating states of affairs by tracking total or average utility. A measure of this sort will have nothing to say about the *shape* of the distribution and so will not tell you by how much the actual distribution diverges from the ideal distribution. For example, consider the following two distributions: (5, 5) and (7, 3). If (5, 5) is the ideal distribution, then (5, 5) is clearly closer to the ideal than (7, 3). Average or total utility has no way of tracking this, however. Both have the same average utility and both have the same total utility, yet the shapes of the two distributions are very different. Because egalitarianism is a comparative notion, it must take shape into account in some way. (And so will theories of comparative desert for example.) In fact, going by total or average utility does not single out one unique distribution as the ideal. If the total amount of well-being in the ideal case to be divided up among persons is 10, then both (5, 5) and (7, 3) look identical from the point of view of justice, unless some other principle is brought in to break the tie.[12] Divergence measures, on the other hand, can measure how far a given actual distribution is from *the ideal distribution* (where the ideal distribution is identified by some other prior method) while paying attention to the shape of a distribution when they measure by how much one distribution diverges

[11]   If we thought of welfare probabilistically, then we can even easier plug it into the developed toolkit for measuring divergence between probability distributions. It seems appropriate for a politician, for example, to think probabilistically when choosing between policies. In this essay, however, we will be dealing with welfare distributions that obtain with certainty and so will not be dealing with probability distributions.

[12]   Sidgwick for example uses equality to break ties in such cases, giving preference to the more egalitarian of the two distributions in cases when both distributions have the same total utility. See Henry Sidgwick, *The Methods of Ethics* 7th edition [1907] (Indianapolis: Hackett Publishers, 1981), p. 417.

from another.[13] This will give due attention to each point in that distribution (i.e. give due consideration to each *person* since each point in the distribution represents the amount of welfare a given person has).

There is, however, more than one possible way to measure divergence between two distributions and which divergence measure is the right one is an open question. One requirement is that the measure satisfies the four constraints we listed above. We find divergence measures attractive not only because they offer a way to measure the injustice of a distribution relative to the ideal distribution (and because they seem to give due attention to each point in the distribution and hence to each person, instead of, say, aggregating the distribution), but also because divergence measures seem automatically to satisfy our four constraints as we will show below in the example below.

One standard measure of divergence between distributions used in information theory is the Kullback–Leibler divergence.[14] This measure, however, was designed to deal with probability distributions and so is not properly suited for welfare distributions. This is because probability distributions always sum up to 1, which means that the sum of probabilities across one distribution will be equal to the sum across any other distribution. For welfare distributions, however, total welfare in one distribution will not necessarily be equal to the total welfare in another distribution. Recall the levelling down objection. In particular, recall the life boat example. The point of the objection is that while it would be nice for everyone to live, regrettably this is not possible. One person must get thrown overboard or everyone dies. It might also be more just if, instead of drawing straws and throwing

---

[13] Divergence measures are not necessarily metrics and so do not measure the distance between two distributions because they lack symmetry: by how much distribution S_1 diverges from distribution S_2 is not necessarily equal to how much distribution S_2 diverges from distribution S_1.

[14] KL-divergence is used on probability distributions, which means that points in the distributions it is applied to add up to 1. KL-divergence is often interpreted as measuring the entropy of one probability distribution relative to another. It can be used, for example, to measure the difference from the data or scientific observations (the ideal distribution) to a scientific theory that tries to account for that data (the actual/ arbitrary distribution). In the case of ideal theories of distributive justice that concern themselves with patterns, e.g. in our case an egalitarian theory, we are trying to do something very similar in spirit: measure the difference from the ideally just distribution (e.g. the ideal egalitarian distribution that maximizes average utility) to the actual distribution (i.e. the current state of affairs).

someone overboard, we could instead subtract the number of years that person had left to live from the total sum of years everyone in the boat has left to live and then divide those years equally. In other words, it might be fairer for everyone in the boat to share the burden equally instead of having one person bear *all* of it. But this isn't possible either. So our only two choices are: everyone drowns or only one person drowns. If we think of the ideally just distribution as one in which everyone lives and, for the case when there are only three people in the boat, represent it as (3.3, 3.3, 3.3), then the case when everyone drowns is (0, 0, 0) and the case when only one person drowns is (5, 5, 0). The latter distribution clearly diverges from the ideal less than the levelled-down distribution. What is even more striking, however, is that the sums across the distributions aren't equal. Total welfare in the levelled-down distribution is 0, whereas in the ideal case it is 10 (and similarly, in the case when only one person drowns, total welfare is 10). This is important because it sets welfare distributions apart from probability distributions and makes standard measures of divergence between probability distributions (e.g. KL-divergence) not suited for our present purposes. Furthermore, normalizing a welfare distribution so it would look like a probability distribution (i.e. so that it would sum up to 1) would miss the whole point we have been labouring to make. If the ideal case in which everyone lives and the levelled down case in which everyone drowns are normalized so that the two distributions both add up to 1, they would look identical! But this, we have argued, is a mistake because what motivates our egalitarian intuitions is a concern with the welfare of each person, whereas normalization and levelling down only pay attention to the shape of the distribution, which violates our constraint that, all other things being equal, pareto superior welfare distributions ought to be preferable to pareto inferior distributions.

Thus, as a working hypothesis, we would instead like to suggest a simpler measure of divergence for the two-person case (which does not demand that distributions be normalized to sum up to 1):

Divergence $D(S_{actual} \| S_{ideal}) = \left(\dfrac{1}{x} + \dfrac{1}{y} \right) - \left(\dfrac{1}{x^*} + \dfrac{1}{y^*} \right)$ between the

ideal distribution (x^*, y^*) and the actual distribution (x, y), where x and y represent portions instead of actual welfare: in other words, x and y are fractions of the total amount of welfare to be divided up under ideal circumstances.[15] In the life boat example, with two people in the boat, the ideal distribution (5, 5) would be $(5/10, 5/10) = (0.5, 0.5)$ because the total amount of welfare (or maybe years) to be divided up in the ideal circumstances is 10. The case (10, 0) when one person lives and the other drowns would then become (1, 0), and the levelled down case would, of course, remain (0, 0). Formally, $x = A/W$ and $y = B/W$, where W is the amount of total welfare to be divided up in the ideal circumstances, A is the amount of welfare the first person actually gets and B is the amount of welfare the second person actually gets. If the ideal distribution were (6, 6) instead of (5, 5), the numbers in any actual distribution would have to be adjusted accordingly before they could be used in this divergence measure. An actual distribution (5, 5) for example would no longer be $(5/10, 5/10) = (0.5, 0.5)$ when represented as percentages of total welfare, but instead would be represented as $(5/12, 5/12) \approx (0.4, 0.4)$ because total welfare in an ideal distribution (6, 6) is obviously 12 because $6 + 6 = 12$.

This measures how far each person's well-being is from the ideal. The closer to zero, the better because the ideal distribution will not diverge from itself at all (i.e. will have zero divergence from the ideal). The following table ranks different distributions using this divergence measure, where the ideal distribution $S_{ideal} = (x^*, y^*) = (0.5, 0.5)$. The distributions are listed from most just to least just in table 1:

Distribution (0.5, 0.5) coincides with the ideal distribution (5, 5) in our initial example and so does not diverge from it at all, which is why its divergence value is zero.

Note that (0.5, 0.6) is not possible because it would mean that the total amount of welfare has exceeded 100%. Another way of

---

[15] The more general form of this divergence measure for the n-person case and which does not presuppose that the ideal distribution is egalitarian is

$$D = \sum_{i=1}^{n} \frac{x_i^*}{x_i} - \sum_{i=1}^{n} \frac{x_i^*}{x_i^*} = \sum_{i=1}^{n} \left(\frac{x_i^*}{x_i} - \frac{x_i^*}{x_i^*} \right) = \sum_{i=1}^{n} \left(\frac{x_i^*}{x_i} - i \right) = \left(\sum_{i=1}^{n} \frac{x_i^*}{x_i} \right) - n, \text{ such that } \sum_{i=1}^{n} x_i^* = 1, \text{ but}$$

not necessarily $\sum_{i=1}^{n} x_i = 1$ since leveling down might be an (inferior) option. The total amount of well-being in the *ideal* distribution is then normalized to sum up to 1 (albeit not for all actual distributions). Divergence D measures the difference from the ideal welfare distribution $(x_1^*, x_2^*, \ldots, x_n^*)$ between n persons to some arbitrary/actual distribution $(x_1, x_2, \ldots, x_n)$, where x_i is the amount of well-being person i actually gets and x_i^* is the amount of well-being person i should get in ideal (i.e. ideally just) circumstances.

Table 1

$S_{actual} = (x, y)$	$D(S_{actual} \| S_{ideal})$	
(0.5, 0.5)	0.00	← Ideally just distribution.
(0.45, 0.45)	0.44	
(0.4, 0.5)	0.50	
(0.44, 0.44)	0.54	
(0.7, 0.3)	0.76	
(0.4, 0.4)	1.00	
(0.2, 0.2)	6.00	
(0.99999, 0.00001)	999997	
(0.5, 0.00001)	999998	
(0.1, 0.00001)	1000006	
(0.1, 0.00001)	1000096	← Least just distribution of those listed in this table.

stating the same point is that were the corresponding welfare distribution (5, 6) possible, then the ideal welfare distribution would be at least (5.5, 5.5) since the total amount of welfare under circumstance would then be at least 5 + 6 = 11. If the total amount of well-being in the circumstance turned out to be even greater than 11, say 12, then the ideal egalitarian distribution would be (6, 6) and (5, 6) would indeed be closer to the ideal than would (5, 5).

The distribution (0.99999, 0.00001) is an approximation to (10, 0), which would result in division by zero and so, using our divergence measure, would result in an undefined divergence value.

Let us see how the measure we have discussed satisfies the four constraints on a measure of approximation to ideal equality. We can see from the above table that the ideal equality is the best given the divergence measure since the divergence is 0. And we can also see that the measure prefers some equalities over some inequalities even though they have less average utility such as the case in (0.45, 0.45) or even (0.44, 0.44) over (0.7, 0. 3). And the measure prefers equal distributions over unequal distributions that have the same average utility. But the measure also prefers (strongly and weakly) Pareto superior distributions to Pareto inferior distributions.

We are not sure if (0.7, 0.3) getting ranked as more just than (0.4, 0.4) is a troubling result. This might, of course, not be the right divergence measure for egalitarian justice and so, as we have noted above, we offer it merely as a working hypothesis because we think it provides a good illustration of how one might go about measuring the divergence of an actual distribution from the ideal distribution and thus having a procedure for choosing the least of all evils when comparing and evaluating non-ideal distributions.

Notice that the principle of equality articulated in the above way will give us some practical guidance even in those circumstances where the ideal equality point is infeasible. It does this by telling us what feasible states are the most just approximations of the ideal equality point and thereby telling us what the least unjust outcome is in the circumstances. So the principle of equality we have elaborated does give us practical guidance even when the ideal cannot be achieved.

The strategy accords with the principle of equality defended in this essay because both the ideal equality and the rule of approximation take structural and well-being considerations into account. The principle of equality articulated here ensures that only equality is the ideal distribution; the importance of well-being ensures that the Pareto superior equality is more just than the Pareto inferior equality. The method also prefers Pareto superior inequalities over Pareto inferior equalities. And the method of assessing departures from equality in terms of divergence from the ideal equality seems highly intuitive.

This seems to us to give exactly the right result. The idea is that there is injustice in an unequal condition when there are no relevant differences between the persons between whom the inequality holds. But, there is less injustice in such an unequal condition than in an equal condition that is strongly or even weakly Pareto inferior.

But this shows how one can think that there is something lost and problematic in efficient inequality, and also think that it does not follow that egalitarians are committed to the proposition attributed to them in the levelling down objection. For that objection to work against an egalitarian principle of justice it is not enough that the egalitarian is committed to the injustice of inequality. The levelling down objection applies to equality only if the egalitarian is also committed to the claim that inequality is worse from the point of view of the principle of equality than a Pareto inferior equality. But it is this last claim that the egalitarian need not and indeed ought not be committed to, as we have argued.

Have we simply changed the question? We have responded to the levelling down objection by defending a principle that seems to avoid it. But is this really what egalitarians are after? Or is it a new principle? We want to defend the claim that it is the right principle of equality. Remember that an essential part of the rationale for the principle of equality involves the claim that more substantial good is better than less. The argument for equality involves this essential premise. What would be the point of equality if this were not so? Given the internal connection between equality and the idea that more is better than less when it comes to the thing equalized and given the argument for equality that we have given, it seems reasonable to hold that this is the proper conception of equality.

Cohen and the difference principle

In chapter 4 of his book *Rescuing Justice and Equality* G. A. Cohen argues against the difference principle on the grounds that it allows inequalities on the basis of arbitrary differences among persons. This argument goes beyond his famous arguments against Rawls's inclusion of incentives to the talented as legitimate bases for inequality.[16] He argues that even if it is not possible to help the worst off without inequality the inequality is unjust. In this essay, we believe we have defended a position that accepts Cohen's conclusion because it argues that all inequalities are unjust. But it also qualifies that conclusion in an interesting way, making some sense of the idea that the difference principle is connected with justice. For we have argued that feasible Pareto improvements over feasible equalities are unjust but they are nevertheless more just than the feasible Pareto inferior inequalities. The reason for this, we have argued, is that the feasible Pareto superior inequalities are closer to the ideal equality in the circumstances than the feasible Pareto inferior inequalities.

One way of describing many of the distributions favoured by the difference principle is as a principle of justified injustice. They are unjust for the reasons Cohen describes. They favour some over others for morally arbitrary reasons. But they can be justified nevertheless because they are superior to the feasible equality. But

---

[16] In chapter 1 of *Rescuing Justice and Equality*.

our point is stronger than this. Our point is also that many of the distributions favoured by the difference principle may be required by principles of justice when we take into account not only the principle of ideal justice but we also take into account principles of how best to approximate justice. On these principles, not only might many distributions favoured by the difference principle be justified; it may also be the case that the distributions favoured by the difference principle are more just than the feasible alternatives. And in this respect many distributions favoured by the difference principle may be required by justice.

We think this addendum to Cohen's position is necessary for the reasons we have stated above. It avoids the levelling down objection while endorsing a pure conception of egalitarian justice. It does so, we believe, in a theoretically satisfying way.

4

INEQUALITY, INCENTIVES AND THE INTERPERSONAL TEST

Kasper Lippert-Rasmussen

Abstract
This essay defends three claims: (1) even if Rawls' difference principle permits incentives to induce talented people to be more productive, it does not follow that it permits inequalities; (2) the difference principle, when adequately specified, may in some circumstances permit incentives and allow that the worst off are not made as well off as they could be; and (3) an argument for incentives might pass Cohen's interpersonal test even if it is unsound and might not pass it even if it is sound.[1]

1. Introduction

In *A Theory of Justice* Rawls famously canvassed a '[principle] of justice for institutions' which he labelled the 'difference principle'. In his so-called 'final statement' of the principle Rawls says that institutions are just only if '[s]ocial and economic inequalities are . . . arranged so that they are . . . to the greatest benefit of the least advantaged'.[2] Rawls thinks that incentives-related inequalities, in the absence of which talented people will choose to be less productive than they could be, are compatible with the difference principle.[3] In Cohen's view, this is not so. He argues with characteristic rigour and ingenuity that such inequalities are inconsistent with: (a) the basic motivation offered by Rawls in support of

---

[1] I thank Paula Casal, Jakob Elster, Christel Fricke, Eline Busck Gundersen, Nils Holtug, Sune Lægaard, Raino Malnes, Søren Flinch Midtgaard, Mike Otsuka, Andrew Williams, and Gerhard Øverland for insightful comments on an earlier draft, which was presented at the Centre for the Studies of Mind in Nature, University of Oslo, January 23, 2008.
[2] John Rawls, *A Theory of Justice* (Oxford: Oxford University Press, 1971; second edition 1999), p. 302/266 (throughout this essay, page references to this work are given, in order, to the first/second editions).
[3] See, however, Samuel Scheffler, 'Is the Basic Structure Basic?' in Christine Sypnowich (ed.), *The Egalitarian Conscience* (Oxford: Oxford University Press, 2006), pp. 102–129, p. 114.

the difference principle, to wit, that inequalities reflecting differential luck are unjust;[4] (b) the existence of a justificatory community of talented and untalented people; and (c) Rawls' vision of a well-ordered society, in which people are motivated in their daily lives by considerations of justice.

The so-called interpersonal test plays an important role in Cohen's critique of Rawls' permissive view of incentives. In this role the test involves imagining a group of talented people presenting to a group of untalented people the putative Rawlsian justification of inequalities: 'Whatever inequalities make you as well off as possible are just. In the absence of our being given extra rewards we will work less hard and you will be worse off. Hence, it is just that we are given extra rewards' (cf. p. 34). The interpersonal setting in which the argument is presented shows that the offered justification fails, because the empirical premise to which the talented people appeal is one which they make true and they cannot justify their readiness to make it true by invoking the difference principle. To the extent that talented people wholeheartedly endorse the difference principle, they will not, in their economic behaviour, hold out for incentives in such a way as to make untalented people worse off than they need be. Cohen concludes that distributive justice may require an egalitarian ethos encouraging talented people to 'accept very high rates of taxation' without withholding labour (p. 70n40).[5]

In Section Two, I argue that the incentives argument for inequality is flawed for a reason which Cohen does not flag: namely, that it ties the existence of incentives to talented people too closely to the existence of inequalities in their favour. Accordingly, even if, contrary to what Cohen argues, the difference principle permits incentives for talented people, in the absence of which they could, if only they intended to, be no less productive, it does not follow that the difference principle permits inequalities in their favour. The argument in this section does not supply premises for the arguments in the ensuing sections. What it does

---

[4]   Ultimately, Cohen thinks that this motivation condemns not only Rawls' application of the difference principle to the issue of incentives but the principle itself: G. A. Cohen, *Rescuing Justice and Equality* (Cambridge, Mass.: Harvard University Press, 2008) pp. 156–161. (All unattributed parenthetical references are to this work.) My concern here is the first issue.

[5]   Here I largely disregard the complication that, for purely self-interested reasons, the wage elasticity of labour supplied by talented people may be zero or negative: see Joshua Cohen, 'Taking People as They Are?', *Philosophy and Public Affairs* 30 (2002), p. 375.

is locate the incentives argument and Cohen's critique of it in a wider dialectical setting that is even less friendly to inequality than that in which Rawls and Cohen tend to locate it. In Section Three, I explore an extension of Cohen's critique of incentives. That critique implies that the difference principle instructs talented individuals to act in certain ways. But this raises the question, which Cohen does not pose, whether the difference principle similarly instructs untalented individuals to act in certain ways – and if so, what these are. I argue, in the light of cases where worse off people fail to make themselves (and others) as well off as possible, that the difference principle is most plausibly specified in such a way that it does not require the talented to make the untalented as well off as possible in all circumstances and may even, in a narrow range of cases, permit incentives. While this specification and its implications are independently interesting, the former (the specification) supplies an important background assumption for my discussion of the interpersonal test in Section Four. There I submit that, despite being unsound, the Rawlsian justification of incentives may pass the test in a range of cases where untalented people bring it about that they are worse off; and that some justifications of incentives, despite being sound, may fail to pass the test. Cohen's interpersonal test is a very telling test, but the justice of distributions and the existence of justifications for inequality passing the interpersonal test are separate issues.

Three preliminaries: in his critique of incentives Cohen has two targets. His 'primary target as a philosopher is a pattern of justification [of inequality]', while his primary target, 'as a politically engaged person . . . [is] the real-world inequality that is actually defended on incentive grounds' (p. 56). As the nature of my sketchy examples below will attest, my concern here is exclusively with Cohen's first target.

Second, I shall stipulate that people are exhaustively divided into two non-overlapping groups: talented people, who, besides being talented, are better off than others unless equality obtains, and untalented people, who, besides being untalented, are worse off unless equality obtains. This assumption is made solely in the interest of simplification and is not intended to suggest anything about the nature, distribution, or causal effect of talents.

Third, a person is talented in the sense relevant here if, and only if, this person's labour-power is in high demand due to higher productivity and this is the result of what, from the perspective of this person, is a matter of brute good luck.[6] A person can be talented in the ordinary sense without being talented in the present sense, e.g. because he is lousy at communicating his extraordinary productive skills. Similarly, one can be untalented in the ordinary sense and yet talented in present sense (pp. 119–120).

2. Incentives without inequality

There is an incentive for a person, P, to do something, A, if, and only if, (P believes that) P's desires will be satisfied to a higher degree if P does A than they will if P does not do A.[7] If all of P's desires are self-regarding, and if self-interest is promoted by the satisfaction of one's self-regarding desires, then P has an incentive to do A if, and only if, doing A serves P's self-interest better than not doing A. To the extent that P has non-self-regarding desires (e.g. if P simply desires that equality obtains) P may have an incentive to do A even if doing A does not serve P's self-interest. Here I am concerned exclusively with incentives deriving from the agents' self-regarding desires.

By definition whether someone has an incentive to do something is a matter of how attractive this course of action is compared to others.[8] Hence, there could be inequality favouring talented people and no incentives for these people to work, or there could be equality *and* strong incentives for talented people to work. Suppose wages vary across jobs and people are taxed solely on the basis of their talents: the greater the talents you have, the more tax you pay. Talented people might then have a strong incentive to work: high wages and no income tax. Yet, if the talent tax revenue is redistributed to worse off people we might still end up with equality. To illustrate a situation of inequality favouring

---

[6] Accordingly who is talented depends on the choices all of us make as consumers: see Kasper Lippert-Rasmussen, 'Publicity and Egalitarian Justice', *Journal of Moral Philosophy* 5.1 (2008), pp. 35–37.

[7] The parenthesized qualification captures a subjective aspect of incentives which, setting aside odd cases, is necessary for incentives to have any motivational effects. Henceforth, I omit this clause and assume that there is no gap between what will satisfy an agent's desires and what the agent believes will do so. 'Desires' is meant to refer to all those items that are normally thought of as pro-attitudes, some of which (e.g. a sense of duty) would not fall under this term in its narrower, everyday meaning.

[8] Accordingly there are no incentives of which it is strictly true that it is 'constitutive of' them 'that they produce inequality' (cf. p. 35).

the talented in which they have no incentives to make an extra effort, we can imagine a society in which there is a talent bonus, so the greater talents you have, the greater bonus you receive; but in which the fruits of labour are taxed away and used to fund the talent bonus. The conceptual independence of incentives and equality implies that even if it is just for a group of talented people to enjoy incentives, nothing follows about whether it is just for them to end up better off than others if they do what they have incentives to do.

There is a special case in which incentives are intimately tied to inequalities: the case in which a person desires to end up better off than others. Here a person has an incentive to do something if he will end up better off than others provided he does that thing. But note, first, that the incentive still lies in the fact that doing what he has an incentive to do is a better option for him than other available options. The fact that doing what he has an incentive to do will leave him better off than others is only contingently related to his having an incentive and is due to the particular content of his desires. Second, to desire to end up better off than others is a special case, in the sense that few people care about their level of income only because they have a desire of that sort. Third, the desire to be better off than others is even harder to square with Rawls' characterization of the just society than the person-wise non-comparative desire to have a greater income. Surely, a person driven by such desires is not a member of Rawls' well-ordered society, manifesting the value of fraternity by not wanting 'to have greater advantages unless this is to the benefit of others who are less well off'.[9]

In discussing incentives, Rawls and Cohen are insufficiently observant of the conceptual independence of incentives and inequality, although they are obviously aware of it. Consider Rawls' suggestion that 'the greater expectations allowed to entrepreneurs encourages them to do things which raise the long-term prospects of laboring class. Their better prospects act as incentives so that the economic process is more efficient, innovation proceeds at a faster pace, and so on.'[10] By 'greater expectations' and 'better prospects' Rawls here means *greater than the expectations* and *better than the prospects of people who do not belong to the entrepreneurial class.* Had he

[9] Rawls, *A Theory*, pp. 105/90.
[10] Rawls, *A Theory*, pp. 78/68.

meant *greater expectations than they would have if they did not do what (in Rawls' view) their better prospects encourage them to do* and *better expectations than they would have if they did not do what makes the economic process more efficient* (etc.), he would not be describing the difference principle's implication that some inequalities are just – which is what he thinks he is doing.[11] But, setting aside the special case mentioned in the previous paragraph, entrepreneurs have an incentive to do whatever makes the economic process more efficient (etc.) independently of the fact that if they do those economically beneficial things they will be better off than others.[12]

Consider next how Cohen states the central question guiding his critique of Rawls' view of incentives. His central question is how to interpret 'the word "necessary" in John Rawls' difference principle. When he [Rawls] says that inequalities are just if they are necessary to improve the position of the worst off, does [should] he countenance only inequalities that are necessary (to achieve the stated end) apart from people's intention, or also, and more liberally . . . , inequalities such as those that are necessary when talented people lack a certain sort of commitment to equality and are set to act accordingly?' (pp. 68–69; cf. pp. 27, 34–35, 51–52, 98–99, 119, 143).[13] This question would make little sense if Cohen were not assuming that incentives are so tightly tied to inequalities that to ask whether the difference principle allows the *inequalities* needed to make the worse off people better off relative to talented people's intentions about how to respond to the absence of incentives is, in effect, to ask whether the difference principle allows the *incentives* required to make the worse off people better off relative to talented people's intentions about how to respond to those incentives' absence. However, by expressing his question in this way Cohen is too concessive. For *even if* the difference principle were not to imply that talented people act unjustly in responding to reduced incentives by electing to reduce the amount of labour they supply, it would not follow that inequality favouring the talented is compatible with the difference principle. It is simply a further question whether the difference principle requires incentives-neutral forms of taxation of talented

---

[11] Rawls, *A Theory*, pp. 78/67–68.

[12] For further support for my exegetical claim, see Rawls, *A Theory*, pp. 151/130–1.

[13] It is clear both from the overall structure of the relevant chapters and from the immediate context of the quoted passage that Cohen is not simply asking an exegetical question about Rawls' text. Hence, the inserted 'should'.

people the revenue of which can be redistributed to worse off people so as to eliminate the inequality otherwise generated by incentives. By way of illustration consider the package of a high-wage rate for jobs requiring special talents, a low marginal income tax rate, and a tax on talents the level of which varies with the level of talents one has and independently of the amount (and kind) of labour one supplies. This may combine strong incentives for talented people to supply their labour (since working more makes them much better off than if they work less) with no inequality (since redistribution through the talent tax neutralizes differences in the relevant distribuendum).

One might concede the correctness of the distinction between incentives and inequality drawn here and still dismiss it as being, though relevant to Cohen's argument, something that can be ignored on two main grounds. First, in practice we cannot fine-tune the tax system so that the combination of a tax on talents and undiminished incentives make the untalented as well off as possible. Hence, we need an egalitarian ethos to 'guide choice within the rules' as a supplement (p. 124). Setting aside Cohen's view concerning the fact-insensitivity of non-derivative principles of justice (here and in the response to the second challenge raised below), we might note that the impossibility of fine-tuning is a feature of the egalitarian ethos too. We might add that if the aim is to encourage collective coordination, in some contexts it may be more effective to introduce tax laws than it is to rely on individuals applying what they perceive to be social norms in a way they believe to be correct. Second, a tax on talents will enslave the talented: they will be forced to employ their talents to maximize their incomes, and thus be able to pay their talent tax without ending up worse off than others.[14] In response to this, note first that, as Cohen points out elsewhere, provided the measure of how well off someone is accommodates the welfare effects of one's work, the slavery here is

---

[14] Rawls makes roughly this objection in his *Justice as Fairness: A Restatement* (Cambridge, Mass.: Belknap Press of Harvard University Press, 2001), p. 158, arguing that a lump sum tax on native endowments violates the priority of liberty, partly because it prevents talented people from being 'able to afford to enter low-paying, though worthy, vocations'. However, it is hard to see the force of this observation given that under virtually any scheme and for virtually any person, including *untalented* ones, there will be worthy vocations that they are unable to afford to enter but would be able to enter under an alternative scheme. Rawls also suggests that we cannot determine people's talents. However, if this is a problem here, surely, it is also a problem in relation to the Rawlsian norm of equality of opportunity enjoining equal prospect for people with the same talent and same willingness to use it.

special in that if the 'slaves' exercise their talents they will end up
no worse off than others (pp. 207–208; cf. Rawls' Aristotelian
Principle). If, despite this, we judge it objectionable, as Cohen
does, for people to be forced to exercise their talents, incentives
without inequality might still be achievable provided we can indirectly tax the talents of talented people who employ their talents
instead of surfing at Malibu beach indirectly without reducing
incentives. We could perhaps do the latter by taxing high-fliers
whose supply of labour, for purely selfish reasons, is not reduced by
increased taxation. Moreover, to respond to the present challenge
I need only claim that it is sometimes possible to have incentives
without inequality *and* without enslaving the talented, e.g. because
the proportion of the population that is talented is high and
endowment-related wage differentials between talented and untalented are small. If this combination is possible in some cases or to
some degree, it is wrong to see the argumentative setting of the
dispute about Rawls' incentives argument as one in which it follows,
if incentives that are not in a strict sense necessary for the talented
to be more productive are just, that resulting inequalities felt in the
absence of compensatory taxation are just. Note, finally, that a
standard tax-based implementation of the lax difference principle
may also force talented people to choose occupations in which they
can exercise their talents (p. 202).

Having separated the justification of incentives and the justification of inequalities in the way I have suggested, I now need to look
again at the way in which Cohen (and others) phrase the question
whether the difference principle justifies inequalities. Even if the
difference principle permits incentives to induce talented people
to be more productive, it does not follow that it permits inequalities
in their favour. Ultimately, however, the argument in this section is
in harmony with Cohen's denial that the difference principle
justifies the kind of inequalities brought about by talented people's
inclination to withhold labour in response to reduced incentives.
Indeed, it supports the same incentives inequality-sceptical conclusion, though on different grounds.

3. The difference principle and the daily lives of
untalented people

Cohen wants to refute the incentives argument. Given that it
appeals to a particular causal hypothesis about how talented

people can affect the situation of worse off people, he reasonably focuses on ways in which the former can affect the situation of the latter. He argues that the difference principle, understood as a principle of just distribution, should be read as saying something along the following lines: an unequal distribution is just if, and only if, (i) there is no alternative distribution under which the least advantaged people are better off;[15] and (ii) there is no such distribution only where its unavailability does not reflect the intentions of talented people to refrain from acting in ways that they are able to act.[16]

If the difference principle applies only to the basic structure of society, and if we understand that structure as, say, a legally enjoined one rendering most of the day-to-day choices of people legally optional, no issue will arise about how the difference principle instructs untalented people to act in their daily lives. However, if we adopt Cohen's understanding of the difference principle, obviously, issues of this sort will arise. In this section I therefore want to ask whether the difference principle can be specified to accommodate the fact that not only the talented, but also the worse off themselves, may influence levels of inequality.[17] There are two situations to consider: those in which the worse off affect their own situation only (call these 'self-affecting' or SA situations); and those in which the worse off affect their own situation as well as that of the talented ('everyone-affecting' or EA situations).

Among SA situations we must distinguish between: those in which the least advantaged are worse off than they need to be because it is true of each worse off person that he is worse off as a result of his own autonomous choice; and those in which this is not so. I shall assume, in cases of the first sort here, that we could have a just distribution even if it is not to the greatest benefit of the least advantaged – the reason being that the unavailability of

---

[15] The difference principle so formulated (1) is silent about the justice of an equal distribution under which everyone is worse off than they would be under an alternative equal distribution and (2) allows inequalities that do not harm the worst off. Presently, Cohen thinks that the motivation underlying the difference principle's focus on inequalities – that inequalities reflecting differential luck are unjust – militates against (2): see note 4 and (pp. 317–318).

[16] Cohen would want to add a clause accommodating a Scheffler-like agent-centred prerogative (p. 61), but this complication is one that I can set aside here.

[17] In point of fact a specification of this kind is provided in the last paragraph of the present section.

the distribution in which the least advantaged are better off reflects the autonomous choice of each of the least advantaged persons to refrain from acting in ways that would render him better off. First, the difference principle is a principle of justice, and arguably one does not act unjustly by autonomously making oneself worse off. If that is right, and setting aside special cases (e.g. in which a worse off person autonomously chooses to fulfil his moral obligation to rescue a better off person from a burning building and knowingly suffers a minor burn in the process), a distribution in which one is worse off solely as a result of one's autonomous choice cannot be unjust.[18] Second, in the present context disambiguating the difference principle in the way suggested ought to be acceptable. For while Cohen does not endorse the difference principle as a fact-insensitive principle of justice, the relevant choice component is part of his favoured fact-insensitive principle of justice; accordingly he should favour a reading of the difference principle that does not condemn situations in which the worse off are worse off through their own (genuine) choice.[19]

Consider now the other kind of SA situation (i.e. situations in which worse off people are worse off partly as a result of the choices of other worse off people). Suppose, first, that each worse off person can affect the situation of exactly one worse off person, except this time around no one can affect how well off he is himself. Suppose, moreover, that each worse off person is worse off than he need be partly as the result of a choice made by another worse off person and not as a consequence of his own choices. Here, the resulting inequality should be condemned as unjust by the difference principle, because the exclusion of the distribution in which the least advantaged people are better off reflects the intentions of the worse off people not to benefit each other.[20] First, behind the impulse underlying the difference

---

[18] For related, though importantly different, views, see Ingmar Persson, 'A Defence of Extreme Egalitarianism', in Kasper Lippert-Rasmussen and Nils Holtug, *Egalitarianism: New Essays on the Nature and Value of Equality* (Oxford: Oxford University Press, 2007), pp. 83–86; Michael Slote, *Common-Sense Morality and Consequentialism* (London: Routledge & Kegan Paul, 1985), chapter 1.

[19] G. A. Cohen, 'Currency of Egalitarian Justice', *Ethics* 99 (1989), pp. 906–44. Whether responsibility-generating, autonomous choices are possible, let alone common, is a question I bypass here.

[20] Like Rawls, I set aside, both here and in the examples below, considerations about moral deservingness.

principle seems to be the idea that luck-induced inequalities are unjust, so if a better off person acts against the spirit of the difference principle in making a worse off person worse off than he need be, why should it be any different if a worse off person makes another worse off person worse off relative to better off people than he need be? Second, at least some of the things which Rawls says, and which Cohen quotes in support of his strict interpretation of the difference principle, would also support the proposed specification of the difference principle. For instance, Cohen writes: 'How could your "nature as [a] moral person" count as "*most* fully realized" when you go for as much as you can get in your markets choices, and merely endorse application of the principle by the government in imperfect moderation of the inequality which the choices of people like you tend to cause?' (p. 75). The parallel challenge vis-à-vis worse off people who refrain from benefiting other worse off people has no less force.[21]

Consider, finally, a situation in which the worse off can affect the situation of other worse off people and – like the talented people in the situation the incentives argument addresses – have incentives to make self-interested choices which will make worse off people even worse off. So suppose that each worse off person has two options: either he keeps 50 for himself and puts 25 into the common pool, or he puts all 75 into the common pool where they will then grow to 100. The common pool will in either case be distributed equally among worse off people, so each person knows that he will get at least 25 from it. Suppose that everyone suspects that quite a lot of people will choose to put all their resources into the common pool, and that nevertheless everyone refrains from doing so, and hence they all end up with 75. Here no worse off person will be worse off through his own choice. Indeed any worse off person who had chosen to act otherwise than he did would have been even worse off. Yet the group of worse off people is worse off partly as a result of the way in which all of its members chose to act.

People act unjustly in selecting the self-centred option, certainly. But the resulting distribution should also be condemned as unjust by the difference principle when its scope extends beyond institutions. It may not be unjust that the group as such is worse off

---

[21] A similar point can be made about the incoherence of the fraternity characterizing a well-ordered society and worse off persons failing to costlessly improve the situation of other worse off people (thereby reducing inequality).

to some extent: after all the group is worse off to some extent as a result of its members chosen acts, so in this respect the present case is analogous to my first case involving individual choice. However, the distribution is unjust to the extent that each worse off person is worse off for a morally arbitrary reason – namely, that all of his fellow worse-off citizens chose the self-centred option.

Now consider two EA cases, and recall that here the choices of worse off people determine how well off they *and* the better off are. In the first case the worse off people choose unanimously to act in such a way that, whatever the better off people do, the better as well as the worse off will be irreversibly worse off than they would have been under an alternative, equal distribution (everyone at 150) the worse off unilaterally rendered impossible. (Suppose worse off people have strong non-self-regarding preferences for the spacecraft-based exploration of other solar systems and unilaterally decided to make sure that massive resources are devoted to that purpose despite leaving everyone worse off.) Here, if the talented insist on incentives for working harder, they, and the worse off, will end up better off than they would if there were no incentives and the talented withheld labour in response (talented at 100 and untalented at 75 instead of everyone at 50). However, the talented and worse off will also end up considerably worse off than they were under the initially feasible equal distribution.

Two questions arise here. Is the resulting distribution unjust for leaving the better off worse off than they need be? Is the inequality resulting from incentives more unjust than the equal one in which talented people work harder without incentives?

Two considerations motivate an affirmative answer to the first of these questions. First, distributive justice has an intrapersonal, (as it were) subjunctive element. That is, it concerns not only how the positions of different people compare with one another, but also how the position of a person compares with what it might have been. This means that if someone, while preserving equality, makes all of us much worse off, this act, as well as the resulting distribution, might be unjust to those who are made worse off unwillingly, even if there is no injustice in our being equally well off. If you decide to engage in a very attractive gamble involving exactly the same prospects and risks for both of us without my consent and we both end up equally, and quite badly, off, I might complain of the injustice of my plight even if I do not think it unjust that you end up no worse off than I do. If by luck I return to the superior level I would have been at had the gamble not been imposed on me, justice will be restored even if you also return to your level.

Second, intuitively, quite what costs justice requires one to bear to improve the situation of another is affected by the way in which that person affects his own situation. Compare the situation in which an initial, equal distribution is knocked out of the set of feasible distributions by an event beyond human control with the situation, described in the previous section, where the untalented are worse off than they need be as a result of their own choice. From the point of view of justice, complaints on behalf of the talented about their burdens in raising the prospects of the least advantaged seem more powerful in the latter case.

These two considerations have a bearing on the justice of the incentives-generated inequality in my example. First, the fact that incentives will bring talented people closer to the level they would have enjoyed in the initially feasible distribution the untalented rendered impossible makes it just for them, pro tanto, to insist on incentives.[22] Second, the fact that the worse off are badly off as a result of their own choice means that the talented need no longer act unjustly in refusing to bear the burden of ensuring that the worse off become better off.

It follows from the line of argument in the preceding paragraph that the difference principle should allow some incentives-related inequalities.[23] Still, this might not rehabilitate the particular kind of incentives argument that Cohen rebuts. This argument holds that incentives are just because incentives are needed to make the worst off better off (p. 35). What might justify incentives, on the present view, is something more complex: that the worse off are worse off

---

[22] 'We may assume that no one is obliged to sacrifice so much that she drops to a level *worse* than what she would be at in an egalitarian society', G. A. Cohen, *If You're an Egalitarian, How Come You're So Rich?* (Cambridge, Mass.: Harvard University Press, 2000), p. 176. A plausible elaboration of this view about reasonable sacrifice would imply that one is never required to sacrifice so much that she drops to a level *worse* than the highest possible equal level when those for whose sake one would be asked to make these sacrifices are those who made the latter level unfeasible.

[23] Arguably, the situation in which this is so is one involving partial compliance with principles of justice and Cohen is primarily concerned with whether the difference principle permits incentives under full compliance. However, the reason that the present situation is one involving partial compliance has nothing to do with talented people's insistence on incentives and nothing to do either with the fact that the present situation is one that would be more unjust in the absence of incentives. The case I present below might be one of full compliance, assuming that one does not act unjustly in failing to benefit oneself.

than they need be as a result of their own choice; and that incentives make better off people – who can, after all, still be pretty badly off – come closer to being as well off as they would have been under the distribution that the worse off unjustly rendered impossible (cf. pp. 403–404). This response, however, points to another problem. For if the critique of the incentives argument does not address difference principle-based justifications of inequality not appealing to the fact that these incentives make the worse off better off, Cohen *might* not be in a position to suggest that equality, though rejected by his socialist critic as a premise, instead reasserts itself as a conclusion (pp. 33–34).

To see, finally, if the difference principle might allow incentives justified at least in part by their making worse off people better off, consider a case which is analogous to Cohen's case of incentives, but in which the incentives benefiting the talented people are needed to induce untalented people to act otherwise. Suppose everyone is equally well off initially (100, 100). We then offer a training scheme. Training is boring but enables one to be more productive. Suppose that, unlike the talented, the untalented will not (although they could) take up this offer unless they receive incentives in the form of entertainment during training. For some reason, however, incentives must be offered to everyone, and the talented get more out of them: they are more easily entertained. Hence, we end up with an unequal distribution favouring the talented (110, 115). Suppose, finally, that if the untalented were to take up the opportunity of training, even in the absence of incentives, everyone would end up equally well off at a level higher than the initial one (120, 120).

If we set aside how well off the untalented people end up, this case is morally analogous to the first case I introduced: since it is the worse off who themselves ensure that they end up worse off than they need be, the difference principle, suitably amended, should not condemn the inequalities introduced by the incentives-cum-training scheme. Moreover, this case differs from my first EA- case in that, arguably, here it really is, in part, the fact that introducing the incentives makes the worse off better off that justifies those incentives. So, arguably, this is a case where the difference principle is compatible with incentives for untalented people that introduce inequalities and are justified, also, by the way in which they affect the worse off.

The claims made in this section suggest we should formulate the difference principle thus: setting aside situations in which the least advantaged have rendered an equal distribution which leaves everyone better off impossible, an unequal distribution is just if, and only if, (i) there is no alternative distribution under which the least advantaged people are better off; and (ii) there is no such distribution only where its unavailability does not reflect the intentions of talented people to refrain from acting in ways that they are able to act *or* where its unavailability reflects the intention of each untalented person to act in ways that make him worse off than he need be. In the situations set aside, the difference principle requires everyone who is not a member of the group of worse off people to make a reasonable effort to act so that worse off people are as well off as possible. Reasonable efforts need not be maximal, but they must appear reasonable in the light of worse off people's efforts with the same aim.[24]

4. The interpersonal test

In the preceding section I considered a number of situations in which the worse off are worse off than they need be as a result of their own choices. I asked how the difference principle should be specified in the light of these cases. I now want to consider whether the incentives argument might pass Cohen's interpersonal test in some such cases. Ultimately, my aim is to clarify the role this test can play in Cohen's critique of incentives.

Cohen's interpersonal test determines 'how robust a policy argument is, by subjecting it to variation with respect to who is speaking and/or who is listening when the argument is presented. The test asks whether the argument could serve as a justification of a mooted policy when uttered by any member of society to any other member . . . If, *because* of who is presenting it, and/or to whom it is presented, the argument cannot serve as a justification of the policy, then whether or not it passes as such under other dialogical conditions, it fails (tout court) to provide a comprehensive justification of the policy' (p. 42).

Cohen argues that the naked incentives argument fails this test. It cannot serve as a justification presented by the talented to the untalented, because the latter might challenge the talented to justify their insistence on incentives – something they cannot do

---

[24] For present purposes I need not elaborate the notion of 'reasonable efforts' further.

if they are only allowed to appeal to the difference principle. The incentives argument can, however, serve as a justification when it is presented by one group of untalented people to another group of untalented people. For in this dialogical setting the presenter of the argument can reject a request for justification of the fact that talented people make the factual premise of the argument true. Hence, dialogical conditions affect the justificatory efficacy of the incentives argument.

Let me clarify the sense in which the incentives argument fails to serve as a justification. Suppose we specify the difference principle as I just did in the last paragraph of Section Three. Given this specification, the incentives argument will fail when presented in the situation Cohen addresses. It will do so because the unavailability of a distribution in which the least advantaged are better off in the absence of incentives asserted in the argument's factual premise reflects the intentions of talented people to be less productive than they are capable of. Accordingly, an argument for incentives that appeals to the difference principle so specified fails *whoever* utters the argument. This is not to deny that there is another sense in which the argument does not fail whoever utters it, for it might vary whether those uttering the argument are entitled to utter it, however sound or unsound it might be. In 'Casting the First Stone' Cohen distinguishes, in effect, between responding to an argument by 'denying . . . [its] inherent soundness' and responding by denying the arguer's right, morally speaking, to make that argument 'in a posture of judgment' without thereby confronting the soundness of the argument.[25] If I unjustly deprive you of all morally permissible means of realizing the most important ambition in your life – an ambition we can assume to be morally justified – I am in no position to argue, in a posture of condemnation, that what you are doing in pursuit of your aim is morally impermissible, even if the argument as such is indisputable. Similarly, a hardened sinner does not have the standing to point indignantly at the misdemeanour of a saintly person. In both cases, 'there are facts about the critic that compromise her utterance considered as, what it purports to be, a *condemnation*'.[26]

This distinction – between criticizing an argument as unsound and criticizing the postured presentation of it by an arguer,

---

[25] G. A. Cohen, 'Casting the First Stone: Who Can, and Who Can't, Condemn the Terrorists?' *Royal Institute of Philosophy Supplements*, 81 (2006), p. 118.

[26] Cohen, 'Casting', pp. 119–120.

whether it is sound or not – allows us to criticize the incentives argument in two ways. As already indicated, once it is made clear what the difference principle says about how individuals should conduct themselves in their daily lives; and when it is emphasized that the incentives argument is meant to establish that inequalities of incentive are fundamentally just and not simply just given the unjust dispositions of some; it can be seen that the argument is unsound. But this unsoundness does not depend on the dialogical setting of the argument, and accordingly it is not necessary to appeal to the interpersonal test to demonstrate the incompatibility of incentive-based inequalities and the difference principle suitably specified.[27] Also, the incentives argument can be criticized in the second mode Cohen describes: that is, to some utterances of the argument it might be replied that the arguer is not in a position, morally speaking, to make that argument. The effectiveness of this criticism, unlike the unsoundness criticism, depends on who presents it. The talented people who make the factual premise true are not in a position to assert it together with a moral principle that condemns their making the factual premise true. What interests me here, especially given the cases introduced in Section Three, are cases where these two criticisms come apart: on the one hand, cases in which the incentives argument is sound and yet talented people are in no position to present it, and on the other hand, cases in which the incentives argument is unsound and yet talented people are in a position to present it.

Here is a case that illustrates the first possibility. Suppose talented people falsely believe that they are able to work harder in the absence of incentives. A group of untalented people, who are aware of the truth of the matter regarding the need for incentives, might respond to the utterance of the incentives argument, by the talented, by conceding that the justification offered is sound; and yet they may take time to explain to the talented why they are not in a position to proffer it given what they believe about their ability to produce more even in the absence of incentives.[28]

---

[27] This redundancy claim is independent of the claim, made below, that in some circumstances worse off people might not be in a position to complain about talented people canvassing the incentives argument for inequality.

[28] One might suggest that the interpersonal test should be specified so that it applies only to situations where the parties to the dialogue have relevant, true beliefs. However, sometimes when people respond to an argument by denying the arguer the right to put it forward they support the putative lack of right on the basis of other propositions the arguer falsely believes.

The second possibility – where the incentives argument is unsound and yet talented people are in a position to present it at least in the sense that no addressee is in a position to complain about their putting it forward – can be illustrated with some of the scenarios I described in Section Three. Consider the third scenario, where worse off people act on the incentive to keep their resources for themselves instead of pooling them. Here worse off people may not be in a position to complain about talented people's making the factual premise of the incentives argument true – partly because they themselves are unwilling to benefit others in the absence of any self-centred incentive to do so (thereby inviting a '*Tu quoque*'-reply), and partly because the extent to which they are worse off than talented people is in part the result of their own actions (thereby inviting a 'You're involved in it yourself'-reply).[29]

Cohen discusses a situation in which talented people might argue that the worse off are not in a position to complain about their putting forward the incentives argument. He imagines the better off appealing to the claim that the worse off, too, would insist on incentives if they were in their (the better off's) shoes. Cohen rejects this reply, partly because the relevant counterfactual claim might be false, and partly because, even where it is true, this would not justify the insistence on incentives by those who are actually better off (p. 61).

However, what one would do in counterfactual situations has a bearing on what others may justly do to one. For example, if I would never help anyone else were I in a position to do so, intuitively, this would reduce the burden justice places on others to help me. And, as Cohen points out elsewhere, there seems to be such a thing as counterfactual *Tu quoque*.[30] In any case, the scenario I am appealing to is not a counterfactual one in which the worse off could make themselves better off and do not, but an

---

[29] There are ways of cancelling the infelicity of putting forward an argument which one is otherwise not in a position to present: Gerald Dworkin, 'Morally Speaking', in Edna Ullmann-Margalit, *Reasoning Practically* (Oxford: Oxford University Press, 2000), p. 184. For instance, were the untalented in the scenario at hand to initially concede that they too are at fault for not improving the lot of other worse off people, they would be in a position to deny the talented the right to canvass the incentives argument. But given that any argument may be challenged in any dialogical setting provided the relevant infelicity cancellers are supplied, the justificatory power of argument will not vary across dialogical settings, when so supplemented; and the interpersonal test works only if such variation is possible.

[30] Cohen, 'Casting', p. 123n.

actual situation in which the worse off can make themselves better off and do not. Nothing in Cohen's discussion of the counterfactual situation bears directly on how we should evaluate this case.

5. Conclusion

The three main claims of this essay are: (1) even if the difference principle permits incentives to induce talented people to be more productive, it does not follow that it permits inequalities favouring the talented; (2) the difference principle, specified to address situations in which untalented people are able to affect how badly off they themselves and talented people are, may in some circumstances permit incentives and allow that talented people do not make the worst off as well off as they could; and (3) an argument for incentives might pass the interpersonal test even if it is unsound and might not pass it even if it is sound.

5

FREEDOM OF OCCUPATIONAL CHOICE

Michael Otsuka

Abstract
Cohen endorses the coercive taxation of the talented at a progressive rate for the sake of realizing equality. By contrast, he denies
that it is legitimate for the state to engage in the 'Stalinist forcing'
of people into one or another line of work in order to bring about
a more egalitarian society. He rejects such occupational conscription on grounds of the invasiveness of the gathering and acting
upon information regarding people's preferences for different
types of work that would be required to implement such a policy.
More precisely, Cohen maintains that the presence versus the
absence of such intrusion explains why such Stalinist forcing of the
talented is unacceptable whereas the progressive taxation of their
income is legitimate. I argue that Cohen's appeal to invasiveness
does not adequately capture the moral repugnance of the state's
conscripting people into work at a given occupation. I propose that
a right to self-ownership, and that which explains such a right,
provides a better explanation than Cohen's of why Stalinist forcing
is objectionable, whereas progressive taxation is not.[1]

In Chapter 5 of *Rescuing Justice and Equality*, entitled 'The
Freedom Objection', G. A. Cohen considers a pair of contrast-
ing cases. In the one case, there is only one possible line of work
– that of producing widgets. Here Cohen maintains that equality
requires an exceptionally talented individual to produce more
widgets per hour while collecting the same wage as those who are
ordinarily talented. In the other case, equality requires someone
with medical talents to abandon her chosen occupation of gar-
dener in order to devote herself to treating the sick as a gainfully
employed doctor. The latter egalitarian demand gives rise to a

[1] I presented an earlier version of this chapter at a conference on G. A. Cohen's
Rescuing Justice and Equality at the University of Reading in April 2007. I thank the members
of the audience for their comments. I am especially grateful to Jerry Cohen for his reply to
my presentation on the day. The chapter has been extensively revised in an attempt to meet
his numerous objections. The brevity of the final product is owing to the fact that half of
the text had to be abandoned in the face of insuperable objections.

freedom of occupational choice objection to which the former does not.

Cohen stipulates that in his widget case labour 'is equally a drag or a joy for everyone' (p. 182).[2] He maintains that 'If, being more talented and having suffered nothing special to acquire her talent, A produces more widgets per hour of comparably repugnant (or unrepugnant) toil than B, then justice forbids paying A at a higher rate per hour' (p. 181). Justice forbids this because an egalitarianism whereby 'people's access to desirable conditions of life is equal' requires that A 'provide greater product than others at the ordinary rate, because she's more able than others and will consequently be as well off as they are (even) if she does so' (p. 182). Cohen writes:

> If, then, A uses her capacity to control how hard she works to secure a higher rate of pay by refusing to produce as many widgets per hour as she could (working no more arduously than B) except at that higher rate, then she strikes a posture that sets her against just egalitarian principle. (p. 181)

Cohen maintains that:

> The egalitarian position's implication sketched in the [preceding passage] is more immediately palatable than another one that I must now bring to the fore. The implication drawn above is comparatively palatable because, by hypothesis, the only difference between A and B is that A is more productive than B *within the same line of work*. Different types of work do not come into the foregoing example, and there is therefore no question of asking A to provide a type of work (as opposed to a quantity of effort and product) that she is unwilling to offer at the ordinary rate . . . (pp. 181–2)

Although the egalitarian position is more palatable, for the reason Cohen offers, in a society in which there is only one type of work, there is nevertheless a significant freedom-based objection to which the realization of equality might give rise even in such circumstances. This is because, even when there is only one type

---

[2] All such references are to *Rescuing Justice and Equality* (Cambridge, Mass.: Harvard University Press, 2008).

of work, there is still the matter of the freedom either to provide work of that one type or not to work at all. To illustrate this claim, let us suppose that the number of widgets each is capable of producing per unit of time is known to all and that it is also general knowledge that widget production is equally burdensome per unit of time for each. Drawing on this knowledge, the managers of the widget factory – let us assume them to be the democratically-elected governing board of a socialist workers' cooperative – might simply refuse to pay A anything other than an egalitarian wage. Assuming that this workers' cooperative is the only widget factory around, then, given Cohen's stipulation that widget production is the only type of work in this society, A will simply be out of a job if she doesn't accept an egalitarian wage. If, however, nobody can survive in the absence of a job, and the members of this workers' cooperative don't need A's contribution in order to produce enough for their own sustenance, then the cooperative will be able simply to wait until A becomes sufficiently hungry that she comes crawling back for a job at an egalitarian wage.[3]

If there are other workers' cooperatives in competition with this one, it might be in the rational self-interest of the members of another cooperative to hire A at an unjustly inegalitarian wage. If, however, all cooperatives adhere to egalitarian principles of justice, then once again A will be forced on pain of starvation to work for an egalitarian wage. So long as individuals have no attractive alternative to gainful employment, it would make sense for an egalitarian state to ban anyone from paying anything other than an egalitarian wage in these circumstances.

Suppose, however, that it is possible for A to hold out for an inegalitarian wage because she is able to survive and get along well enough even in the absence of any gainful employment. She would be able to do so if the government adhered to the unconditional provision of a generous basic income. We can see now that an unconditional basic income will frustrate the realization of equality insofar as it enables the talented to withhold their labour unless they receive an inegalitarian wage. An unconditional basic income has, however, been defended on grounds of freedom,

---

[3]   Cohen supposes that refraining from work is not an attractive option when he writes: 'Suppose that only A can do job j – it requires special talent – and job j is, moreover, the least disagreeable job that A can do. . . . Then no special incentive will be required to induce A to do j' (p. 202).

prime among which is the freedom from being forced by necessity to work.[4]

One's commitment to such an unconditional basic income will depend, at least in part, on whether one thinks it is more important for everyone to have the freedom to choose not to be employed or more important to restrict the opportunities of talented individuals to frustrate the realization of equality by withholding their labour altogether. Someone who places priority on the latter consideration over the former will favour a conditional means-tested basic income over an unconditional one – where the relevant condition is the lack of those talents that will enable one to be gainfully employed.

Now let us suppose that, as is actually the case, the extent of peoples' talents is not transparent to all. If, for the sake of equality and at the cost of freedom from toil, an egalitarian opts for a conditional means-tested, rather than unconditional, basic income, then he opts for something that will require intrusive investigation to determine whether or not the potential recipients of this basic income are capable of gainful employment. It is, however, on grounds of the intrusiveness of gathering and acting upon information regarding people's preferences for different types of work that Cohen rejects the 'Stalinist forcing' of people to engage in one or another line of work for the sake of realizing equality. More precisely, Cohen maintains that the presence versus the absence of such intrusion explains why such Stalinist forcing of the talented is unacceptable whereas the progressive taxation of their income is legitimate. I shall expose some difficulties with this explanation in the remarks to follow.

In resisting the Stalinist policy of forcing people into certain lines of work for the sake of equality, Cohen says the following about an ideal case in which everyone is moved to follow the egalitarian ethos:

> In a truly just society, with full compliance, taxation on behalf of equality would not need to be coerced. But there might still be a state, that is, a central organizing body, that proposes a tax

---

[4]   See, for example, Robert van der Veen and Philippe Van Parijs, 'Universal Grants versus Socialism: Reply to Six Critics', *Theory and Society*, 15 (1986): 723–57, at pp. 727 and 757 n. 12. Cohen offers a critique of such a freedom-based defence of an unconditional basic income in G. A. Cohen, 'Notes on the Universal Grant Proposal', *Basic Income Studies*, 1 (2006): 1–3.

structure of egalitarian inspiration around which people would voluntarily coordinate. Informational problems would prevent the state from similarly (noncoercively) legislating job allocation. But if it could do so, under a properly prerogative-informed egalitarian principle, then I would see nothing wrong with that. (p. 221)

But then, a few lines down, he says the following about a non-ideal case in which citizens are unmoved by the egalitarian ethos:

[Stalinist conscription of people into the optimal occupation would] assert a control over your behavior that exercises a knowledge of the intimacies of your personality, what pleases you, what bores you, and so forth. That control means manipulation of people on a scale to which only a crazed libertarian could think income tax comparable. Even if (a further extravagant assumption) people did not mind their whole inner economy being known by officials, they would have to be meeker than human to not mind that knowledge being used to tell them what to do. (pp. 221–2)

The former passage says that there is nothing wrong with the state's making use of knowledge of the intimacies of people's personalities in order to inform them of what they ought to do in the ideal case, whereas the latter says that it is objectionable to make use of this knowledge in order 'to tell them what to do' in the non-ideal case. So what Cohen is saying is that there is nothing wrong with making use of intimacies of people's personalities in order to let them know what they ought to do when they want to do what egalitarianism requires, but that this use becomes objectionable when they don't want to do what egalitarianism requires and the informing them of what to do also takes the form of a command.

Cohen assumes, for the sake of argument, that people do not mind 'their whole inner economy being known by officials' in the non-ideal case. He maintains that, being human, they would nevertheless mind being told what they ought to do. Presumably they would mind this because, unlike those in the ideal scenario, they 'do not affirm and act upon the correct [i.e., egalitarian] principles of justice' (p. 221). But why should the fact that they would be bothered provide a justification for the state's refraining from telling them what they should do when their being bothered is a consequence of their false anti-egalitarian convictions? Suppose, to draw an analogy, that nobody minded if state officials deployed a sophisticated data mining technique that unearths all and only those occasions on which employers are moved by sexism in their hiring decisions, thereby revealing many more cases of discriminatory hiring than was hitherto possible. Presumably Cohen would think it unobjectionable to use this information in order to draw the attention of justice-loving anti-sexists to their (presumably unconscious) sexism in their hiring and to recommend corrective measures that these employers would gladly embrace. Would he have reason to object, by contrast, if the state deployed this technique in order to order sexist employers to correct their discriminatory hiring practices? Even if such people would have to be 'meeker than human to not mind' the use of the information obtained from that technique in order to tell them what to do, why should we be bothered by the fact that they mind? They wouldn't mind if they had appropriately non-sexists attitudes. Assuming that it is possible for them to school themselves out of their sexist attitudes, why should we object to the discomfort they feel as the result of these attitudes if they choose not to reform them? Perhaps if they are incorrigibly sexist, we should take into account the fact that they mind. But shouldn't this simply be weighed in the balance against the injustice that would be visited upon the victims of sexist hiring practices if these practices are not prevented?[5]

Suppose now, to return to the Stalinist proposal under review, that someone is bothered by the state's command to engage in a particular type of work because he is committed to falsely inegalitarian principles of distributive justice. One might not be prepared to go so far as to say that such recalcitrance deserves

---

[5]   It is worth recalling that, in a different context, Cohen endorses an 'offensive tastes' objection to welfare egalitarianism, which he characterizes as follows:

> The offensive tastes criticism of welfarism is that the pleasure a person takes in discriminating against other people or in subjecting others to a lesser liberty should not count equally with other satisfactions in the calculus of justice. From the point of view of justice, such pleasures deserve condemnation, and the corresponding preferences have no claim to be satisfied, even if they would have to be satisfied for welfare equality to prevail. (G. A. Cohen, 'On the Currency of Egalitarian Justice', *Ethics*, 99 (1989): 906–44, at p. 912.)

Note that Cohen draws no distinction between those who can and those who cannot help but have their offensive tastes. Presumably he thinks such preferences have no claim to be satisfied even if they are incorrigible.

condemnation to the degree that sexism does. Nevertheless, based as it is on mistaken ethical convictions and damaging as it is to the least well off, this recalcitrance does not appear to ground a decisive objection to the state's so-commanding him.[6]

In the light of these observations, Cohen might retreat to the claim that the mere fact that a state's policy 'exercises a knowledge of the intimacies of your personality' is objectionable quite apart from the fact that people object to being told what to do because they are insufficiently moved by a commitment to egalitarian justice. It might be thought that the mere exercise of knowledge of these intimacies involves an intrusion upon people's privacy. If, however, Cohen retreats to this claim, then he will have to retract the first of the two passages quoted above. Recall that this passage asserts that if state officials could overcome the informational problems that prevent them from ascertaining which lines of work it would be optimal for people to pursue from the point of view of equality, then there would be 'nothing wrong with' their letting them know what jobs they ought to pursue, given the assumption that people are moved by, rather than resistant to, an ethos of egalitarian justice. There would, however, be something wrong with this if the mere exercise of knowledge of the intimacies of people's personalities involves an intrusion upon privacy.

Even if we grant that the mere fact that Stalinist conscription exercises a knowledge of such intimacies is sufficient grounds for its rejection, a further problem with Cohen's line of resistance to occupational forcing remains, which I shall now spell out. Cohen writes that:

Coercive progressive taxation can be justified on the egalitarian welfarist ground that *on average* welfare is higher the more

---

[6]   In his reply to an earlier version of this chapter, Cohen advanced the view that it would be unjust to force an inegalitarian into a different occupation because it is not

legitimate to impose on people ideas of *justice* with which they can reasonably disagree. . . . In other words, one cannot 'suppose that all the urgency and dignity of justice applies to one's own political interpretation of justice' (Williams, *In the Beginning was the Deed*, p. 125), even if one thinks it correct. So one can't coerce the disbeliever in equality. ('Reading: Reply to Mike Otsuka', manuscript, pp. 13–14)

A problem with this reply is that, in ch. 5, Cohen 'qualmlessly allow[s]' (p. 221) the coercive egalitarian taxation of the incomes of disbelievers in equality, yet he is in no position to deny that that would also be the imposition on people of a particular interpretation of justice with which they could reasonably disagree.

wealth a person has: we only need confidence in the averages, we need not invade individual psyches, to tax on a welfarist basis.

Suppose one wanted people to work harder, or more hours than they currently choose to do. Then the Stalinist procedure would be to order them to do so. But that rides roughshod over people's preferences, and if, to avoid that, one investigates those preferences individually, to produce a policy that is sensitive to important variations among people, then the "invasion of the inner economy" objection resurfaces. (p. 222)

My objection to this line is that Cohen's appeal to invasiveness does not adequately capture the moral repugnance of the state's conscripting people to work at a given occupation. To see why it does not, let us suppose that no such invasive investigation is necessary because it is manifest who has what talent and the preferences regarding work of those with any given talent are uniform and common knowledge: e.g., it is common knowledge that all those with a talent for socially productive medical surgery would prefer to be (socially unproductive) basket weavers or butchers, that all those with a talent for socially productive negotiation would prefer to be (socially unproductive) poker players, etc. Stalinist conscription of people into socially productive lines of work would, intuitively, still be objectionable in these circumstances, although resistance to such forcing could not here be based on the objection that the state would need to engage in an invasive investigation of people's inner economies in order to implement this policy.[7]

So what would it be based upon? One very tempting answer is that such conscription would be a violation of people's rights of self-ownership. One need not invoke the full-fledged and distinctively libertarian right of self-ownership that implies the rights to sell one's organs or to sell oneself into permanent slavery. Rather,

---

[7] Even if the state need not engage in an invasive *investigation* to reveal this information, might the mere fact that this policy draws on non-invasively obtained information about the likes and dislikes of different types of people ground an objection? I think not. In setting various taxes, fees, fines, and criminal penalties, the state is already rightly sensitive to already available information regarding the sorts of things that are likely to deter the types of people who are disposed to engage in the particular activities that the state seeks to deter.

one can point to a violation of the more universally accepted control-rights component of self-ownership in order to resist Stalinism.

To illustrate: Consider Nozick's case in which half of the members of society are two-eyed and the other half are blind. At least if we assume that it is medically feasible and can be done safely and painlessly, an unconstrained egalitarianism would imply that the two-eyed each transfer one of their eyes to the blind. If they would refuse, then the only way to realize equality would be through the coercive interference of the state. In this particular case, one need not be a crazed libertarian to think that basic, fundamental rights of control over one's own body stand in the way of the state's seizing sighted individuals and forcing them each to give up an eye. Such forced eye transplants would, for example, violate the basic liberties endorsed by the non-libertarian Rawlsian. In particular, they would violate the 'freedom of the person, which includes freedom from psychological oppression and physical assault and dismemberment'.[8] Most would be inclined to say of this case that, not only is there no legally enforceable moral duty to give up an eye, but that one does not have an unenforceable moral duty to do so either. In other words, refraining from such sacrifice falls within our Schefflerian personal prerogative to depart from equality.[9] Cohen maintains that each of us has some such prerogative – i.e., moral permission – to pursue his personal projects at the expense of the realization of equality. Since such a prerogative simply carves out moral permissions, it could not exempt us from being forced to do that which it remains morally impermissible to refrain from doing because it is our moral duty to do. There are, moreover, forms of sacrifice less extreme than eye transplants that plausibly fall beyond the reach of our personal prerogative to decline and within the realm of our moral duty to perform, yet which it would nevertheless also be an injustice legally to enforce. A pint of blood might plausibly be described as something that it is our unenforceable moral duty to donate from time to time. Here we have

---

[8]   John Rawls, *A Theory of Justice*, rev. ed. (Cambridge, Mass.: Harvard University Press, 1999), p. 53.
[9]   See Samuel Scheffler, *The Rejection of Consequentialism* (Oxford: Oxford University Press, 1982). See also Michael Otsuka, 'Prerogatives to Depart from Equality', in Anthony O'Hear, ed., *Political Philosophy*, Royal Institute of Philosophy Supplement, 58 (Cambridge: Cambridge University Press, 2006), pp. 95–111.

a right to do wrong, which is to say that we have a right not to be forced to do our moral duty. The right not to be forced to give a pint of blood is plausibly grounded in our moral general control rights of self-ownership over our own bodies.

In cases involving the sacrifice of labour rather than limb or other body part, the thought is also compelling that one has a right not to make sacrifices to the point of equality. We might be morally required to render relatively non-burdensome services to those in dire need. The legal coercion of some such services via threat of imprisonment, as in the case of easy rescue laws, might also be unobjectionable. It would, however, be unjustifiable to use such means to force able-bodied individuals – and such individuals would have no moral duty – to devote every afternoon to the provision of caretaking services that enhance the welfare of the ill and infirm to the point where it is no less great than that of the able-bodied.[10] Such labours would fall within the personal prerogative of the able-bodied to decline. As in the case of body parts, there is also a range of services to the less well off that are not so onerous as to fall within the scope of our personal prerogative to decline yet which it would also be unjustifiable to force us to engage in. We would have an unenforceable moral duty to provide such services. Perhaps a duty to volunteer at least an afternoon every other weekend to serving the needy would plausibly be described as such. Once again, the right not to be conscripted to provide such services is plausibly grounded in our moral general control rights of self-ownership.[11]

---

[10] See Michael Otsuka, *Libertarianism without Inequality* (Oxford: Oxford University Press, 2003), ch. 1, sec. II. See also Otsuka, 'Prerogatives to Depart from Equality'.

[11] Cohen maintains that the affirmation of a 'species' of self-ownership would stymie his 'ethical solution' to the freedom of occupational choice objection to the realization of equality. On this proposed solution, an optimal level of equality is realized without violating freedom of occupational choice when each is inspired by his ethical commitments and/or fellow feeling to freely choose the optimal type of work that it is his egalitarian moral duty to engage in. According to Cohen, the affirmation of a species of self-ownership would stymie this solution by grounding the claim that 'it is an oppressive denial of the doctor-gardener's aspiration to freedom to expect her to become a doctor at unenhanced pay' (p. 213). I understand a right to self-ownership to be a moral immunity from coercive interference. Such immunity extends to the protection of unethical behaviour: the right of self-ownership implies a right not to be forced to do one's duty in certain circumstances such as those involving the donation of blood or labour that I have mentioned in the main text above. I think, moreover, that it is reasonable and non-oppressive to expect a person to do her duty. (This is not to make the stronger claim that social penalties such as ostracism or shaming could never rise to the level of oppression). Therefore the species of self-ownership to which I appeal does not stand in the way of Cohen's ethical solution.

Such control rights are especially well-tailored to the task of explaining why one has good grounds to reject Stalinist occupational forcing, where such grounds do not also defeat the case for the progressive taxation of income that egalitarians such as Cohen endorse: rights of control over mind and body stand in the way of the state's conscripting individuals on pain of imprisonment into particular occupations, yet they do not also block the taxation of income from labour.[12]

Control rights of self-ownership do not, however, fully explain what's wrong with Stalinist forcing of people into those occupations that are optimal from an egalitarian point of view. This is because such rights do not stand in the way of all such restrictions upon occupational choice that are intuitively highly objectionable. Most anyone who objects to people being forced into a given occupation by means of the imprisonment of those who defy conscription orders would also object to people being forced into a given occupation by means of making their access to those worldly resources necessary for their survival conditional upon their taking up that line of work. Unlike the former method, the latter method of forcing would not constitute any infringement of self-ownership.[13] Nevertheless, these two sorts of forcing appear to be similarly objectionable not just in their magnitude but also in their nature. This suggests that there is an explanation of our aversion to Stalinist conscription that lies at a deeper level than the control rights of self-ownership to which I have appealed.

Hints of such a more fundamental explanation can, I think, be found in the following pertinent remarks of Warren Quinn:

Whether we are speaking of ownership [of objects] or more fundamental forms of possession [of one's own mind or body], something is, morally speaking, his only if his say over what may be done to it (and thereby to him) can override the greater needs of others.

. . . The moral sense in which your mind or body is yours seems to be the same as that in which your life is yours. And if your life is yours then there must be decisions concerning it that are yours to make – decisions protected by negative rights. One such matter is the choice of work or vocation. We think

---

[12] See Otsuka, *Libertarianism without Inequality*, pp. 15–22.
[13] See *ibid.*, ch. 1, sec. IV.

there is something morally amiss when people are forced to be farmers or flute players just because the balance of social needs tips in that direction. Barring great emergencies, we think people's lives must be theirs to lead. Not because this makes things go best in some independent sense but because the alternative seems to obliterate them as individuals. This obliteration, and not social inefficiency, is one of the things that strikes us as appalling in totalitarian social projects – for example, in the Great Cultural Revolution.[14]

The above passage is drawn from Quinn's defence of negative rights and their priority over positive rights, where he spells out the former as 'claim rights against harmful intervention, interference, assault, aggression, etc.' and the latter as 'claim rights to aid or support'.[15] Yet Quinn's objection to forced labour – namely, that our lives would not be ours to lead if our vocation or occupation were determined solely by the greater needs of others – applies when our particular choice of occupation is forced by the prospect of starvation through lack of access to any worldly resources as well as when it is forced by the prospect of being imprisoned for disobeying conscription orders. Infringements of our rights to sustenance, including our rights to access to the world as well as to the aid or support of others, can be just as effective a means of imposition of the designs and wills of others upon us as infringements of our rights of bodily integrity that protect us against seizure and incarceration. In neither case would we end up with sufficient say over how our own lives are led.

One might wonder whether the above explanation justifies anything more than an immunity from coercive interference with activities that fall within the sphere of those moral permissions that constitute our personal prerogative to refrain from doing that which realizes equality.[16] We need an explanation that extends beyond this sphere. We need an explanation of why we also have a right not always to be forced to do that which we have a moral

---

[14] Warren Quinn, 'Actions, Intentions, and Consequences: The Doctrine of Doing and Allowing', *Philosophical Review*, 98 (1989): 287–312, at pp. 308–10.

[15] *Ibid.*, p. 306.

[16] Note that in motivating his belief in such a prerogative, Cohen appeals to the facts that 'individuals indeed have their own lives to lead' (p. 11) and that 'each person [has] the right to be something other than an engine for the welfare of other people' (p. 10). Hence he appeals to considerations that are akin to those that Quinn invokes in objecting to forced labour.

duty to do: i.e., an explanation of a moral immunity from coercive interference, where such immunity extends to the protection of behaviour that is contrary to our moral duty. (Recall my examples above of unenforceable moral duties to give blood or services.) This is admittedly a harder task than that of explaining why we have a right not to be forced to refrain from doing something that we are morally permitted to do because it falls within the sphere of our prerogative.[17]

Difficult as this task may be, it should now be clear that the objection to Stalinist conscription on the grounds that it violates self-ownership is underpinned by a more general objection to forced labour, whether or not that labour is forced by self-ownership-violating (threats of) incursions upon one's person or by the non-self-ownership-violating blocking of access to that which is necessary to sustain oneself. It is, moreover, possible to morally distinguish forced labour of either sort from the progressive taxation of income by drawing on now-familiar explanations as to why, contra Nozick, the latter is neither itself forced labour nor morally on a par with it. It is one thing to determine how people will spend each of their working days by forcing them into a particular job. It is quite another to apply a progressive schedule of taxation upon their income while leaving them free to choose how they will earn this income. It is a credible complaint that our lives are in a very significant respect no longer ours to lead as we choose if we are subjected to a policy of the contemplated Stalinist sort that determines the nature of the tasks in which we will be engaged during every working day. No comparable charge can plausibly be raised against the progressive taxation of our income. We can contemplate less onerous forms of occupational forcing that allow us to select from among a range of occupations rather than limiting us to a single one. We can also contemplate more onerous schemes of taxation such as an inescapable lump sum head tax whose magnitude is determined by one's level of talents.

---

[17] Cohen makes some progress with this difficult task when he writes:

it is not true that there is no point in a freedom to choose between *a* and *b* when only *a* is morally permitted. Suppose *b* is letting someone die and *a* is saving her at little expense to me, or suppose *a* is helping an old lady across the street and *b* is not helping her. Then my freedom to choose between such alternatives matters enormously, even though *b* is morally forbidden: the measure of how much the relevant freedom matters is . . . how outrageous it would be for the state to recruit me to these tasks. The value of freedom lies in the absence of coercion itself, not in the absence of legitimate moral demands that, being legitimate, cannot be absent. (p. 195)

At some point, the scheme of taxation will become as onerous as the occupational restrictions. But that does not vitiate the initial contrast between being forced into a particular job and having one's income taxed at a progressive rate.[18]

---

[18] Cf. Scanlon: 'It may be true, as Nozick claims, that there is a continuum of interferences extending from taxation to forced labor, each foreclosing a few more options than the preceding. But the fact that there is such a continuum is no reason why we must be indifferent between any two points along it.' (Thomas Scanlon, 'Nozick on Rights, Liberty, and Property', *Philosophy and Public Affairs*, 6 (1976): 3–25, at pp. 7–8.) For further resistance to the claim that taxation of income is on a par with forced labour, see Otsuka, *Libertarianism without Inequality*, ch. 1, sec. II.

6

COHEN TO THE RESCUE!

Thomas Pogge

Abstract
Cohen seeks to rescue the concept of justice from those, among whom he includes Rawls, who think that correct fundamental moral principles are fact-sensitive. Cohen argues instead that any fundamental principles of justice, and fundamental moral principles generally, are fact-insensitive and that any fact-sensitive principles can be traced back to fact-insensitive ones. This essay seeks to clarify the nature of Cohen's argument, and the kind of fact-insensitivity he has in mind. In particular, it distinguishes between internal and external fact-sensitivity – that is, whether facts are referenced in the content of the principle, or must otherwise be the case in order for the principle to apply at all. Cohen himself seems likely to endorse *internally* fact-sensitive fundamental principles. This leads to a discussion of Cohen's Platonism about moral principles and the extent to which his arguments cover all its rivals.[1]

It is not often that philosophers do something urgent and important, and it is heartening then to find an intrepid philosopher rescuing, in a single book, two prominent damsels in distress: Justice and Equality. Civilization saved by a timely intervention! Since I have reported earlier on Cohen's rescue of Equality,[2] let me here focus on his rescue of Justice.

Well, actually, what gets rescued here is not justice, really, but the concept of justice (2, 279).[3] Cohen's mission is not to overcome actual injustices or to get them recognized for what they are, but to ensure that in debating such issues we properly understand when we are discussing justice and when something else.

---

[1] For very helpful comments on drafts of this chapter, I am much indebted to Paula Casal, Brian Feltham, Michael Otsuka, Matt Peterson, Andrew Williams and Jerry Cohen himself.

[2] 'On the Site of Distributive Justice: Reflections on Cohen and Murphy' in *Philosophy and Public Affairs* 29/2 (Spring 2000), pp. 137–169.

[3] All page references in the text are to G. A. Cohen: *Rescuing Justice and Equality* (Cambridge, MA: Harvard University Press, 2008).

The concept of justice is an evaluative and normative concept whose employment is guided by certain substantive principles. Following Cohen's practice, I use the word 'principle' throughout in the sense of 'normative principle,' which I understand to be any general statement about how features of the world that agents can influence – conduct, character, social rules and attitudes, states of affairs – ought to be shaped. There is disagreement among philosophers about which substantive principles are correct. Cohen's rescue does not take sides in such disagreements, but concerns a deeper, conceptual issue.

Cohen introduces this issue by dividing philosophers into two camps on the basis of their meta-ethical stance about principles of justice and, really, moral principles generally. Those in the first camp – the majority, he thinks (20, 231) – believe that there are some correct moral principles and that all of them are fact-sensitive. The philosophers in the other camp, Cohen included, hold that some such principles are fact-insensitive. These latter philosophers are also said to believe that any fact-sensitive principles can ultimately be traced back to fact-insensitive principles: that 'fact-insensitive principles are at the summit of our normative convictions' (20).

Cohen's distinction between fact-sensitive and fact-insensitive principles is tricky and will occupy us for much of this essay. Basically, that a principle is fact-sensitive means that its endorsement relies on certain facts. For example, the difference principle is fact-sensitive for Rawls if his commitment to it relies on the fact that it would not allow excessive inequalities.

Cohen makes two moves against the philosophers in the first camp. He argues that they are really committed to fact-insensitive principles – in his own catchy mantra: 'all principles that reflect facts reflect facts only because they reflect principles that don't reflect facts, and the latter principles form the ultimate foundation of all principles, fact-reflecting principles included' (254). In addition, he proposes that only such fact-insensitive principles can be accepted as ultimate and thus deserving the title of principles of justice. This is the celebrated rescue of the concept of justice: We are to accept as a *conceptual* truth about principles of justice that they hold regardless of any and all facts, and we should therefore deny fact-sensitive principles that noble appellation. Fact-sensitive principles can be 'rules of regulation' (253) whose application in a certain factual context is appropriate if, and only if, genuine (fact-insensitive) principles of justice entail that they should be applied in this factual context. With Cohen's rescue accomplished, the next edition of John Rawls's bestseller will bear the endearing title *A Theory of Regulation* and will have nearly all occurrences of the word 'justice' replaced (cp. 304–05). It will then feature the 'two rules of regulation' and perhaps ascribe to all citizens an 'inviolability founded on regulation that even the welfare of society as a whole cannot override.' Rawls is not alive to witness this rescue of 'justice' from his text; but someone will have to tell Sam Freeman.

Before we assign this delicate task, perhaps we better have a look at Cohen's argument. Why should it be true that anyone committed to at least one fact-sensitive principle must therefore also be committed to at least one fact-insensitive principle? Cohen's basic argument is clear and straightforward. It has three premises (236–37):

1. 'Whenever a fact F confers support on a principle P, there is an explanation *why* F supports P, an explanation of how, that is, F represents a reason to endorse P' (236).

Cohen disarmingly admits that he has no argument for this premise, but 'it strikes me as self-evidently true, under a properly unrestricted understanding of what would qualify as such an explanation' (236).

2. 'The explanation whose existence is affirmed by the first premise invokes or implies a more ultimate principle, commitment to which would survive denial of F, a more ultimate principle that explains *why* F supports P' (236).

Cohen adds that: 'For this second premise my defense is simply to challenge anyone who disagrees to provide an example in which a credible and satisfying explanation of why some F supports some P invokes or implies no such more ultimate principle' (236).

Cohen offers no canonical statement of the third premise. The basic idea is this. The first two premises assert that, for any principle P supported by facts F, there is a 'more ultimate' principle P_1 such that (i) P_1 explains why F support P and (ii) P_1 holds regardless of whether F obtain or not. Now P_1 must be either fact-insensitive or fact-sensitive. If P_1 is fact-insensitive, then we have reached the desired conclusion, we have traced back P to a fact-insensitive principle. On the other hand, if P_1 is fact-sensitive, then premises 1 and 2 can be applied once more in order to find an even more ultimate principle P_2 that holds regardless of one of the facts supporting P_1. Premises 1 and 2 guarantee that we can continue doing this, moving from any fact-sensitive principle P_n, to a less fact-sensitive higher principle $P_{(n+1)}$ that holds regardless of one of the facts supporting P_n. Premises 1 and 2 do not guarantee that this iteration terminates. This assurance is provided by premise 3 which – bearing in mind the explanation I have provided – might be formulated as follows:

3. Iteratively applied to any fact-sensitive principle, the elimination of facts terminates in a wholly fact-insensitive principle (which holds regardless of *all* facts).

Cohen gives a helpful example for the kind of iterative process that, he asserts, can always be relied upon to show that endorsement of a fact-sensitive principle involves a commitment to some fact-insensitive principle (234–35): Many assert the principle '*we should keep our promises*' (*P*). Some may be committed to *P* as an ultimate moral principle, regardless of any and all facts. These people are already in Cohen's camp. He therefore addresses himself to the residual: to those who hold *P* as a fact-sensitive principle. These interlocutors will, in support of *P*, adduce at least one (purported) fact, for example, that '*only when promises are kept can promisees successfully pursue their projects*' (*F*). But why, Cohen asks them, should this fact help justify *P*? For the adduced fact to be a reason for *P*, people's successfully pursuing their projects must be something to be promoted. This is the new principle P_1, which Cohen's interlocutors hold regardless of *F*. Some of them may be committed to P_1 as an ultimate moral principle, regardless of any and all facts. This puts them in Cohen's camp; and he can then focus his attention on the remaining others who adduce in support of P_1 another fact, for example that '*people can achieve happiness only if they are able to pursue their own projects*' (F_1). Here Cohen will ask again why they take F_1 to justify P_1. His remaining interlocutors find themselves compelled to respond with a moral principle, '*people's happiness should be promoted*' (P_2), which they are committed to regardless of F_1. Does this clinch the case for Cohen? Not quite yet. For

some might base P_2 on the (supposed) fact that promoting people's happiness expresses our respect for them [F_2]. But then they must hold principle P_3, namely, that we ought to express our respect for people, which, if itself based on a fact, is based on the fact that people possess what are thought to be respect-meriting characteristics [F_3]. The relevant basic fact-free principle P_4 may then be: one ought to respect beings, human or otherwise, who have the relevant characteristics. Note that P_4 is immune to denials that human beings, or any beings, have the relevant characteristics. To be sure, P_4 is inapplicable if no beings have such characteristics, but that certain beings *do* have such characteristics is nevertheless no ground for affirming P_4 (235).

The moral of this story is that, just as Cohen's recursive interrogation technique has forced the reluctant interlocutors in his story to accept that they are committed to a fact-insensitive principle – if not P, then P_1 or, if not P_1, then P_2 or, if not P_2, then P_3 or, if not P_3, then P_4 – so he can force anyone into the same acceptance, so long as they are committed to any principle at all. In short: Whoever is committed to a principle must be committed to a fact-insensitive principle.

Let us look closely at the final step in the debate Cohen imagines, the moment of final victory. The last remaining interlocutors have confessed their commitment to P_3, that we ought to express our respect for people, but still resist Cohen's conclusion that they must therefore be committed to some fact-insensitive principle. They try to resist this conclusion by insisting that they take P_3 to be fact-sensitive, namely supported by the fact that people have certain (respect-meriting) characteristics. Now our hero strikes his final blow, to be replayed here in slow motion. The interlocutors have accepted a narrow, conditional ought: that, insofar as certain facts obtain, one ought to act in such-and-such a way. But this really commits them to an unconditional ought: that one ought to act in such-and-such a way whenever those same facts obtain. Once again in somewhat more logic-like notation:

For all X, if X has the relevant characteristics, then it ought to be the case that I respect X.

This is the conditional ought embedded in the interlocutors' view that F_3 supports P_3. Cohen then infers that these interlocutors must be committed to this universal, unconditional ought:

It ought to be the case that, for all X, if X has the relevant characteristics, then I respect X.

Cohen's final blow strikes me as entirely successful. The defenders of the first camp have been overwhelmed. But is this not a Pyrrhic victory? This worry can best be explained by distinguishing two senses in which a principle can be fact-sensitive. In one sense of this expression, a principle can be fact-sensitive *in its content*: when the directive it gives is conditionalized on one or more facts (the principle gives a certain directive to its addressees in contexts in which those facts obtain and does not give them this directive in other contexts). Such a principle might take a form like *'one ought to do A whenever certain facts F obtain'* or *'it is permissible to do A in contexts of type C'*. I call a principle *internally* fact-sensitive when it so conditionalizes its directive upon facts. A principle is internally fact-*in*sensitive, then, when its directive is not conditionalized upon facts.

In the other sense of this term – Cohen's – a principle can be fact-sensitive *in its range*: when its holding is taken to be conditional on one or more facts (the principle is endorsed for contexts in which those facts obtain and not endorsed for other contexts). Such a fact-sensitive commitment might take a form like: Whenever certain facts *F* obtain, the principle *'one ought to do A'* holds; or: in contexts of type C, the principle *'it is permissible to do A'* holds. I call a principle *externally* fact-sensitive when its endorsement is conditional on certain facts. A principle is externally fact-*in*sensitive, then, when it is endorsed for any and all factual contexts.[4]

Cohen speaks of fact-sensitivity in the latter, external sense. This shows that he thinks of principles as attached to particular persons: as normative beliefs rather than as detached normative propositions. One cannot tell from the content of a principle – *'one ought not lie'*, say – whether it is fact-sensitive in Cohen's sense. It may be externally fact-sensitive for some people, who endorse it specifically for certain factual contexts, and externally fact-insensitive for others, who endorse it for all contexts (whatever the facts may be).

Evidently, a principle can be fact-sensitive in both ways at once. For example, someone may endorse the principle *'rational beings are permitted to choose childlessness when by doing so they would violate no promise'* specifically for contexts where such rational beings belong

---

[4] The words 'conditional' and 'conditionalized' in this and the preceding paragraphs are to be understood in the sense of a *sufficient* condition, not in the sense of a necessary condition.

to a species that is not under threat of imminent extinction. This example displays internal fact-sensitivity in that the principle grants permission only to those who would violate no promise by remaining childless. This example also displays external fact-sensitivity in that the principle is endorsed specifically for factual contexts in which the agent's species is not under threat of imminent extinction.

Moreover, the two kinds of fact-sensitivity are intersubstitutable. Thus, the fact-sensitivity of the moral view just expressed can be wholly internalized, resulting in the principle *'rational beings are permitted to remain childless when doing so would violate no promise and they belong to a species that is not under threat of imminent extinction'.* And this same fact-sensitivity can be wholly externalized, resulting in a principle – *'rational beings are permitted to remain childless'* – endorsed specifically for contexts where such rational beings have neither made a contrary promise nor belong to a species under threat of imminent extinction.

We can now state more succinctly why the first camp of philosophers lost the battle. They held that there are principles and that all of these principles are externally fact-sensitive. They did not realize that external fact-sensitivity can be reformulated as internal fact-sensitivity: that their commitment to some externally fact-sensitive principle can be paired with a commitment to an externally fact-insensitive but internally fact-sensitive principle. These commitments are essentially equivalent and one cannot reasonably resist the latter commitment once one has endorsed the former. Exploiting this fatal vulnerability, Cohen achieves his victory. We saw this in his sample dialogue where he transformed his interlocutor's externally fact-sensitive principle – *'treat any person with respect'*, which this interlocutor takes to hold for dealings with anyone possessing the relevant (respect-meriting) characteristics – into an externally fact-insensitive but internally fact-sensitive principle: *'treat with respect anyone who has the relevant (respect-meriting) characteristics'.*[5]

---

[5] Cohen's crushing defeat of his imaginary interlocutors prompts the question: How dumb are his colleagues? Has a majority of philosophers with an opinion on the question Cohen is raising really failed to see the simple point that fact-sensitivity can be internalized? Does his laborious argument – establishing that those committed to any principle are thereby committed to some externally fact-insensitive principle – really show something actual philosophers have denied? I don't think the actual philosophers Cohen seeks to challenge need deny his simple conclusion. To reach them, Cohen must strengthen its consequent: Those committed to any principle are thereby committed to some externally

Why do I call this a Pyrrhic victory? Because Cohen's meta-ethical triumph comes without the announced rescue of justice. Cohen's interrogation technique wins the day, because there is nothing to the reshuffle from external to internal fact-sensitivity. This is good for Cohen because his imagined interlocutors must confess that, *malgré eux*, they are indeed committed to some (externally) fact-insensitive principle. It is bad for Cohen because his interlocutors can so easily reclaim what Cohen sought to deny them: the concept of justice. All they need do is reformulate their principles so that any external fact-sensitivities are internalized.

How can Cohen block this escape? One obvious move is to raise the bar by legislating that, to count as a genuine principle of justice, a principle must be both externally and internally fact-insensitive. Cohen does not make this claim. It would be difficult to defend, mainly because it would rule out of contention nearly all the principles anyone has ever held or proposed. *'Avert pain'* seems to be among the survivors. But as soon as this directive is sensitized on the characteristics of those beings whose pain may be avertable, the principle becomes internally fact-sensitive. The agent is then directed to consider facts about the complexity of the mental life of the beings whose pain she can avert and to prioritize the averting of pain that would be suffered by more complex organisms.[6] At any rate, there is no need to examine such desperate moves unless and until someone actually makes them. Cohen, at any rate, seems disinclined to make them. His recognition of P_4 – *'one ought to respect beings who have the relevant [respect-meriting] characteristics'* – as an ultimate principle is evidence for this because P_4 directs its addressees to consider certain facts, namely whether beings they encounter do or do not possess the relevant characteristics. And his endorsement of an egalitarian principle of justice – *'one ought not, modulo a personal prerogative, take more wages than the worst off save where such wages are required to compensate for special burdens'* (cf. 401) – is further evidence insofar as its directive, even if further ultimatized, requires attention to facts about the welfare of others. Fully spelled out and ultimatized,

---

fact-insensitive principle *of a certain comprehensive kind*. I believe that Cohen does indeed aim for this strengthened conclusion but, as we will see, he lacks the additional argumentative resources to support it.

[6] To be sure, one might try to circumvent this problem by changing the principle to *'avert quain'*, where 'quain' is defined as pain weighted according to the mental capacities of the being suffering it. But this device does not avoid internal fact-insensitivity but rather expresses it in a gimmicky way.

this egalitarian principle presumably also makes reference to
further facts about those other welfare-capable beings.[7] Thus
Cohen may want to exclude certain animals from the comparison
class and perhaps also beings on distant planets or humans living
in distant ages. In these ways, reference to facts is once more built
in and – unless Cohen wants to rescue the concept of justice also
from himself – such internal fact-sensitivity cannot then be for
him incompatible with the status of a genuine principle of justice.[8]

Here is another move Cohen might make to block the escape.
This move turns on the notion of explanation which appears
in the first two premises of his argument. Cohen might say that
explaining an external fact-sensitivity requires more than just inter-
nalizing it.[9] Something like this is perhaps hinted at by his curious

---

[7]   For a systematic exploration of how an egalitarian principle, however formulated,
leads to implausible conclusions when extended to other species, see for instance, Peter
Vallentyne, 'Of Mice and Men: Equality and Animals' in Nils Holtug and Kasper Lippert-
Rasmussen, eds.: *Egalitarianism: New Essays on the Nature and Value of Equality* (Oxford:
Oxford University Press, 2007).

[8]   Though this paragraph seems to fit most of Cohen's text and, especially, his acceptance of P_4 as ultimate, his 231n2 leaves me worried. He writes there that, to count as
ultimate, a principle must have 'an intelligible meaning' regardless of what the facts are.
What does this mean? Does the principle '*avert pain*' have an intelligible meaning in every
universe where decisions are made? Cohen can say yes: It means that if there were
pain-sensitive beings in that universe, then decisions should be aimed to avert pain from
these beings. But read in this way, the constraint is trivially satisfied. A more plausible
reading would have the constraint require that the words used in the principle must have
application in all possible worlds. But what principle can possibly satisfy this constraint?
What words are there whose meaning can reach across all possible worlds? What is the
ultimate principle explaining the special respect one owes one's mother? Or does this get
explained away as an instrumentally justified rule of thumb that serves welfare equalization? Even if it does, is welfare equalization an aim that can meaningfully inform all
decision-making in all possible worlds? Other worlds can be *very* different from ours: There
may not be sufficiently separable individuals. Life-spans may be dramatically unequal. And
conceptions of the good may be so radically diverse that it seems ludicrous to affirm what
Cohen's egalitarianism requires: that the relational predicate 'is better off than' can
meaningfully be applied to each and every pair of individuals and that the relational
predicate 'is greater than' can meaningfully be applied to each and every pair of welfare
differentials. (Though less than cardinal, the welfare metric Cohen's view presupposes is
more than ordinal: Talk of more or less egalitarian distributions presupposes an interval
scale.)

[9]   This is suggested when Cohen writes that affirmations of the fact-insensitive principles
he is willing to recognize as ultimate principles of justice are 'logically prior' to affirmations
of any fact-sensitive principles that they, in conjunction with appropriate facts, might
support (247). I don't know what Cohen means by 'logically prior' here. But I assume this
is supposed to designate an asymmetrical relation that does not obtain in cases of mere
reshuffling of fact-sensitivity. (A relation R is asymmetrical just in case aRb entails not-bRa.)
I know of no plausible sense of 'logically prior' in which the affirmation of the principle
'*one may remain childless in circumstances C*' is logically prior to the affirmation, for circumstances C, of the principle '*one may remain childless*'.

ascent from P_3 to P_4. He states both P_3 and F_3 in terms of 'people' but then states P_4 in terms of 'beings, human or otherwise.' Now to be sure, P_4 does not, in any intuitive sense, *explain* why the 'relevant characteristics' should be respect-meriting (P_4 just invokes these characteristics in the same bald way as P_3 had done). But P_4 does go beyond P_3-whenever-F_3 by covering non-human beings as well. So Cohen's idea might be that, while rules of regulation may just cover one kind of context (here: one biological species), genuine principles of justice must cover more than that (how much more?) in a coherent way.

But what if Cohen's last surviving interlocutors had been convinced that being human is a necessary condition for meriting respect? Even then, Cohen might say, their ultimate principle would have provided fuller coverage by making that conviction explicit. While P_3-whenever-F_3 says nothing about what respect, if any, is owed to non-humans, an ultimate principle such as P_4 must resolve this question, or so Cohen might say. He could then add that, to count as ultimate, a principle must resolve *comprehensively*, i.e. for any conceivable factual contexts, whether its directive applies in this context or not.

We get to something like this point by understanding Cohen's recursive interrogative technique as forcing, at each dialectical iteration, not merely an upward but also an outward move: The interlocutor says that certain facts F_n support a certain principle P_n. Cohen presses the interlocutor to explain why. This forces the interlocutor to reveal her commitment to a principle $P_{(n+1)}$ that is both higher than P_n (by being F_n-insensitive) and more comprehensive than P_n by covering also contexts in which F_n do not obtain. $P_{(n+1)}$ must cover more ground than P_n because it must explain why P_n holds when F_n obtain and not otherwise. Cohen's relentless interrogation thus drives his interlocutors not merely upward, to ever more fact-insensitive principles, but also outward, to principles that cover an ever larger range of possible factual contexts. When this process terminates (as it must, thanks to Cohen's third premise), the interlocutor has been shown to be committed to a principle that holds whatever the facts may be, in all possible worlds and contexts.

That Cohen seeks to commit his interlocutors to such a morality spanning all possible worlds is suggested also by his discussion of utilitarianism and slavery. The discussion begins with an aptly-named Objector A who worries that, by endorsing utilitarianism, we may be committing ourselves to instituting slavery. Cohen

imagines a Defender of utilitarianism responding that, given
the facts of this world, utilitarianism would never actually entail
the questionable prescription. Even if this response is factually
accurate, and known to be so, it leaves unsatisfied Objector *B*: 'I
oppose utilitarianism because it says that if circumstances were
such that we could maximize utility only by instituting slavery,
then we should do so, and I do not think that would be a good
reason for instituting slavery' (264). To this objection, the
Defender can respond: 'I am not endorsing utilitarianism for the
unreal circumstances you imagine. I am endorsing it for this world
where, as we have found, slavery is never part of the happiness-
maximizing arrangement of human affairs.'

Cohen does not accept the Defender as a utilitarian:

> our ultimate convictions . . . include a hostility to slavery that is
> not utilitarianly based, a hostility, be it noted, that is shared by
> the soi-disant utilitarian who thinks it necessary to cite the facts
> to silence objector *A*. And that hostility to slavery expresses the
> fact-free conviction that no beings characterized as human
> beings happen to be characterized should be in a relationship
> of slavery to each other (266).

This comment plainly assumes that the Defender's morality covers
other possible worlds, including ones in which maximizing happiness and avoiding slavery are sometimes incompatible. Given
this assumption, Cohen's comment can be rationalized as follows:
If the Defender were a true utilitarian, then she would endorse
happiness maximization for all possible worlds and thus hold that
it should take precedence over slavery avoidance in scenarios
where the two are incompatible. There would then be no point
for her to stress the fact that one of these worlds, ours, happens to
be one in which happiness-maximizing arrangements always avoid
slavery. That she *is* stressing this fact shows that she is not really
committed to happiness maximization taking precedence over
slavery avoidance.

The Defender can dispute Cohen's assumption and what
he derives from it. She can say that her morality covers the world
we are in, with its facts, options and real possibilities. This is a
world in which (she is convinced) slavery is never happiness-
maximizing. In this world, therefore, no choice need ever be
made between happiness maximization and slavery avoidance.
This fact reassures her about her commitment to utilitarianism as

a morality for this world. She is grateful for being spared the choice. But this gratitude signals no commitment about what the choice should be if it had to be made. It does not, *pace* Cohen, imply any moral commitments about other possible worlds.[10]

Cohen's neglect of this possibility in the cited passage is related to an unclarity in his notion of (external) fact-sensitivity. That a principle, *P*, is *fact-sensitive* is said to mean that *facts give us reason to affirm P* (20), that *P reflects facts* (231), *responds to facts* (229), *depends on facts* (20), is *grounded in facts* (229), *supported by facts* (239–40), *based on facts* (237), *justified by facts* (238), *fact-bound* (20), *fact-infested* (287), *fact-reflecting* (254), *fact-supported* (20). The unclarity this wealth of expressions leaves unresolved is this. On a broad understanding, a fact-sensitive principle is one that is taken to hold *whenever* certain facts obtain: the facts are a sufficient condition for the principle's holding. On a narrow understanding, a fact-sensitive principle is one that is taken to hold *just in case* certain facts obtain: the facts are a necessary and sufficient condition for the principle's holding. On the narrow understanding, the principle is taken not to hold in the absence of the relevant facts. This understanding is suggested most strongly by the synonyms *depends on facts* and *is grounded in facts*. On the broad understanding, it is merely not the case that the principle is taken to hold when the relevant facts do not obtain. While Cohen assumes the Defender's commitment to be narrowly fact-sensitive (takes her to reject the utilitarian principle for contexts in which it would conflict with slavery avoidance), this commitment may actually only be broadly fact-sensitive (the Defender merely fails to endorse the utilitarian principle beyond the home context).

On the narrow understanding, the two predicates 'fact-sensitive' and 'fact-insensitive' are contraries, not contradictories.[11] For there are *three* possible kinds of cases: (1) The

---

[10] There is another, more straightforward way of showing that Cohen overreaches when he attributes to the Defender 'a hostility to slavery' and 'the fact-free conviction that no beings characterized as human beings happen to be characterized should be in a relationship of slavery to each other.' The Defender may think it necessary to cite the facts simply because she believes that *the objectors* will find them reassuring. She may want to reassure Objector *A* that, in this world, a commitment to utilitarianism never has the implication *A* dreads. And she may want to reassure Objector *B* that the hypothetical circumstances *B* imagines lie outside this world and therefore beyond the intended range of her morality.

[11] That two predicates are contraries means that, if one is true of an object, then the other must be false of this object and it is not the case that, if one is false of any object, then the other must be true of it. 'Bachelor' and 'unmarried' are contraries because it is impossible to be both but possible to be neither (namely an unmarried woman). That two

commitment to P is fact-insensitive (P is taken to hold regardless of any and all facts); (2) the commitment to P is narrowly fact-sensitive (there are facts such that P is taken to hold when they obtain and not to hold otherwise); (3) the commitment is neither fact-insensitive nor narrowly fact-sensitive (there are facts such that P is taken to hold when they obtain and there are other facts such that it is left open whether P holds when they obtain). The broad understanding of fact-sensitivity conglomerates the last two kinds of cases into one disjunctive kind. Thus, 'broadly fact-sensitive' (kinds 2 and 3) and 'fact-insensitive' (kind 1) are contradictories. Since Cohen clearly wants his distinction to be exhaustive in the realm of principles, we must ascribe to him the broad understanding of 'fact-sensitive.'[12]

Once this broad meaning of 'fact-sensitive' is appreciated, the explanation that a devotee of a fact-sensitive principle is required to provide need not take the form of explaining why this principle holds when certain facts obtain and not otherwise. Actually, the explanation wrested from such a devotee *cannot* take this form if it is to explain a commitment of kind 3. Consider such a case where, say, I am committed to P holding in the basic factual context of our world (F) and am not committed either way with regard to P's holding or not holding in other factual contexts ($-F$). When Cohen questions me about the (broad) fact-sensitivity of my principle, I can explain it without appeal to a more ultimate and more comprehensive principle, and this in diverse ways: I can say I have not thought through those $-F$ contexts and am therefore suspending judgment on whether P or some other principle applies there. I can say that the meaning and significance of the terms in which P is couched is interwoven with the basic standing

---

predicates are contradictories means that, if one is true of an object, then the other must be false of this object and, if one is false of an object, then the other must be true of it. 'Married' and 'unmarried' are contradictories because it is impossible to be both and impossible to be neither. (It may be objected that many things, for example trees and numbers, are neither married nor unmarried. My example assumes that these predicates do not apply in such cases, that it is not false but senseless to call the number 3 unmarried.)

[12] I have already done this above in explicating what it is for a principle to be externally fact-sensitive. I took this to mean that its endorsement is conditional on certain facts: whenever these facts obtain, the principle is taken to hold. I took this *not* to mean that whenever these facts do not obtain, the principle does not hold. I have explicated what it is for a principle to be internally fact-sensitive in an analogous way. I took this to mean that this principle makes its directive conditional on certain facts: whenever these facts obtain, that directive is valid. I took this *not* to mean that whenever these facts do not obtain, that directive is invalid.

features of this world and that it makes no sense, therefore, to extend *P* to *-F* worlds. I can say that I find it absurd, and morally offensive, to extend my moral principles to beings and life contexts that I have not experienced do not really understand. We will examine some of these explanations in a moment. What matters now is merely that, even if Cohen is right to think that any devotee of any fact-sensitive principle owes him an explanation of its fact-sensitivity, he cannot conclude therefrom that this explanation will unearth this devotee's commitment to a more ultimate and more comprehensive principle.

If Cohen uses 'fact-sensitive' and 'fact-insensitive' as contradictories, then he must reckon with cases of kind 3, as exemplified in the preceding paragraph. He must reckon with an interlocutor who does not have a view about how principles vary systematically with factual world context – a view that might be captured by more ultimate principles. This interlocutor may be willing to explain her reluctance to extend her morality to other factual world contexts. She may, for instance, offer her conviction that her morality – all of it – should reflect, or respond to, the basic factual context of this world. But she will protest the spin Cohen puts on her view in his statement of the fact-sensitivity thesis: 'our beliefs about matters of normative principle, including our beliefs about the deepest and most general matters of principle, should reflect, or respond to, truths about matters of fact: they should, that is, – *this is how I am using "reflect" and "respond to"* – include matters of fact among the grounds for affirming them' (231, italics in original). Our interlocutor protests because Cohen is here presuming to legislate the meaning of the words used by his opponents. She will reply: 'I do not think it makes sense to extend moral principles to factual contexts that are deeply alien to the one we live in. Thus I take my principles to reflect, or respond to, the basic factual context of this world. On your definition of my words, I come out believing that basic facts about this world are among my *grounds* for affirming the principles I hold. But this characterization is false or at least misleading. I am not judging that my principles would be less fitting or less well-grounded outside the basic factual context of this world. On the contrary, I deny that we are in a position to make such judgments, one way or the other, about how well or poorly these principles fit remote possible worlds.'

Though Cohen is committed to censuring commitments of kind 3 as manifesting a failure of 'clarity of mind' (245–47), most of his text seems oblivious to such cases. But there is a one-page afterthought that introduces such cases as 'a further vagary' (246) and illustrates them with a well-chosen example:

> As a matter of fact, zygote/fetuses become progressively more babylike as they proceed toward birth. But suppose things were different. Suppose, for example, that they were initially more babylike, and regressed to a less and less babylike condition until the day before they are born, when they undergo a spectacular humanization. Then it could not be a reason for not aborting two days before birth that the fetus was already babylike. I think that might throw us into normative turmoil. Our norms are formed under the factual constraint that fetus-age goes with fetus-level-of-development, but since our norms are indeed so formed, we don't know what to say when asked what their ultimate warrant is.

> It is true that we don't need to know what that warrant is, for practical purposes, but (in my view) philosophy's role is not to tell us what we need to know (in that sense), but what we want or ought (for nonpractical reasons) to know (246–47).[13]

Despite its marginal placement, this passage goes to the heart of the divide between Cohen's Platonism[14] and its philosophical alternative which tends to be discussed under the (often ill-defined) *constructivism* label. Those wearing this label are not typically lazily neglecting to unify their moral views about the various factual contexts by tracing them back to ultimate principles that cover all possible worlds. Rather, most of them seem to be kind-3 types who are reluctant to try to cover, with their moral principles, factual contexts substantially different from our own, like the described outlandish context of regressing fetuses. Cohen insists that our morality ought (for non-practical reasons that remain undisclosed) to cover that context. It is then curious that he describes the divide between him and the constructivists in these terms: 'Oxford people of my vintage do not think that philosophy can move as far away as Harvard people think it can from pertinent prephilosophical judgment' (3). We have seen how far Cohen is moving away from pertinent pre-philosophical

---

[13] See also his response to Josh Cohen (267–68).

[14] 'I have found it necessary to reach up to the pure concept of justice' (xvi). See also Cohen's pertinent discussion of Plato (291–92).

judgment. He holds that we should seek to justify all our moral judgments by the 'ultimate warrant' of fact-free principles that cover all possible combinations of facts and hence all possible worlds. If you don't have such ultimate principles – from which you can derive a sound answer for worlds in which fetuses become ever less babylike during gestation and sound answers for every other moral questions arising in any other possible universe (cf. note 7) – then your moral judgments, however correct, are unwarranted. If you are not even seeking such ultimate principles, then you better surrender the concept of justice to Cohen's rescue mission: 'Until we unearth the fact-free principle that governs our fact-loaded particular judgments about justice, we don't know why we think what we think just is just' (291).[15]

This statement is not a pertinent pre-philosophical judgment. Nor is it backed by argument. It's just a bit of good-natured bullying that cannot make up for the fact that all the great argument Cohen marshals is trained on those whose commitments exemplify kind 2. Cohen does not explore, let along engage, the reasons there might be for modesty about the range of one's moral principles. Let us do a little such exploration here.

According to Cohen, we are to investigate a priori what the essential nature of morality is (256–57, 272). This investigation unearths moral principles. Such principles are not analytic (true by virtue of the meaning of the words they contain). So they are synthetic: informative with respect to the choices we face. We can think of synthetic a priori principles as subjective, as commitments this or that person happens to have. Or we can think of them as objective, as correct or incorrect, perhaps knowably so. If we think of them as objective, then we need to explain in virtue of what such principles are either correct or incorrect. This was Kant's question: How is synthetic a priori knowledge possible? Kant gives an answer that covers synthetic a priori theoretical knowledge (of causal interdependence, geometry, arithmetic) and synthetic a priori practical knowledge (categorical imperatives). Cohen does not share Kant's principles, but he does share Kant's belief

---

[15] Remarkably, there is not one example in this book of an ultimate principle Cohen endorses. His egalitarian directives (cited above in the text near note 5) are not general enough to settle how they apply to animals, beings on distant planets or humans living in distant ages – let alone how they apply in very different possible universes. By his own standard, Cohen may not know why he deems just the directives he issues to his readers.

in the objectivity of morality and does not rule out Kant's explanation of how such objectivity is possible (257n39).

Now the objectivity that Kant's explanation supports is not the objectivity of Plato's realism, which conceives statements about pure justice to be true or false in virtue of a wholly mind-independent reality of forms. Rather, Kant held that synthetic a priori (theoretical or normative) propositions are objectively true or false in virtue of certain mental faculties of the being who is entertaining these propositions. Here is a statement of this view regarding the objectivity of propositions about the geometry of space:

> Space is nothing but the form of all appearances of outer sense. It is the subjective condition of sensibility, under which alone outer intuition is possible for us. Since, then, the receptivity of the subject, its capacity to be affected by objects, must necessarily precede all intuitions of these objects, it can readily be understood how the form of all appearances can be given prior to all actual perceptions, and so exist in the mind a priori, and how, as a pure intuition, in which all objects must be determined, it can contain, prior to all experience, principles which determine the relations of these objects. It is, therefore, solely from the human standpoint that we can speak of space, of extended things, etc. If we depart from the subjective condition under which alone we can have outer intuition, namely, liability to be affected by objects, the representation of space stands for nothing whatsoever.[16]

Kant's explanation of how certain geometric features of the world can be objective entails then that these same features are also, in another – 'transcendental' – sense subjective or 'ideal.' This subjectivity consists in their being features of the world as we (humans) experience it, features that are objective 'solely from the human standpoint.' On Kant's account, these geometric features are necessary and universal, displayed by anything that can possibly be an object of experience for us. Yet they are also non-universal in that there might exist beings whose sensibility differs

---

[16] Immanuel Kant, *Critique of Pure Reason* [1787], transl. Norman Kemp Smith, New York, St. Martin's Press, 1964, page A28=B42.

from ours.[17] If we could encounter them, such beings would appear three-dimensional to us. But neither they nor we would appear three-dimensional to them.

All this applies *mutatis mutandis* to Kant's justifying explanation of the possibility of moral principles that are synthetic a priori and objective. Someone who accepts this explanation – and Cohen certainly provides no alternative – might then make two points to Cohen: First, there is a fact-sensitivity that you do not consider. All our moral judgments and principles depend on the fact that we are beings endowed with reason, beings whose mental activity is structured in certain ways. This is a fact-sensitivity that we cannot transcend. Second, this fact-sensitivity is in one sense harmless. For it does not limit the reach of our morality, which can still be extended to any and all decisions in any and all conceivable universes. But does it make sense so to extend it? Does it make sense to apply our moral principles to beings whose mental life is profoundly different from ours so that the basic structure of our moral thinking is incomprehensible to them and the basic structure of their decision-making incomprehensible to us? One can plausibly answer this question in the negative and therefore decline to extend one's morality beyond beings whose mental life has the general features we associate with the notion of reason. If this reluctance is plausible, it furnishes a counter-example to Cohen's mantra[18] and one that he does nothing to debunk.

We find an analogous reluctance closer to home, when the objectivity of certain principles is explained by their being well-integrated fixed-points in some culture's value system. Just as on Kant's view some principles are a priori relative to a certain kind of mental activity ('reason'), so on this view some principles are a priori relative to a certain collective way of life. Realizing this, participants in this collective way of life may be reluctant to extend some of their principles beyond it. For example, a Korean woman might hold that one ought not contradict one's parents. But, realizing that the Korean way of life, which she fully approves, is in this regard different from those of other cultures, she may still be reluctant to pass moral judgment, one way or the other, on a

---

[17] Peter Strawson memorably describes such beings in *Individuals: An Essay in Descriptive Metaphysics* (London: Methuen, 1959).

[18] 'All principles that reflect facts reflect facts only because they reflect principles that don't reflect facts, and the latter principles form the ultimate foundation of all principles, fact-reflecting principles included' (254).'

British woman contradicting her father – and even more reluctant to search for some fact-free ultimate principle that explains her range-bound principle and fits all possible worlds (cf. note 7). Her reluctance poses another challenge to Cohen's mantra. To be sure, I am not endorsing this challenge, nor do I claim that Cohen cannot meet it. My point is simply that Cohen's defense of his meta-ethical view is incomplete because he focuses his arguments on one group of opponents while ignoring various others.

Let me conclude with some remarks on what I find the most crucial issue in this meta-ethical terrain. Cohen holds that the role of moral and political philosophy is to tell us what we ought, for non-practical reasons, to know about what is right and wrong, just and unjust (247). Rawls expresses the opposite view:

> The search for reasonable grounds for reaching agreement rooted in our conception of ourselves and in our relation to society replaces the search for moral truth. . . . The task is to articulate a public conception of justice that all can live with who regard their person and their relation to society in a certain way. And although doing this may involve settling theoretical difficulties, the practical social task is primary.[19]

Cohen agrees that some principles ('rules of regulation') are subject to revision when they do poorly in regard to the practical social task. But he holds that there are ultimate principles exempt from this test, which define the practical social task against which rules of regulation are to be assessed. We can challenge this view by asking what we should do when we find that our commitment to a principle that we regard as ultimate is counterproductive in this world, so that what this principle values would be better served if we were committed to some other principle instead. Can this fact be a reason to revise our commitment?

Cohen says, often and loudly, that the answer is no. But where is the argument? – Let me make the challenge more concrete by sketching the case for an affirmative answer with the help of an example.[20] Suppose we hold some ultimate principle entailing

---

[19] John Rawls, *Collected Papers*, edited by Samuel Freeman (Cambridge MA.: Harvard University Press, 1999) page 306. This passage comes early in the essay 'Kantian Constructivism in Moral Theory.'

[20] This example is drawn from my fuller discussion of this question in 'The Effects of Prevalent Moral Conceptions,' *Social Research* 57/3 (Fall 1990), 649–63.

that abortion in our world is a heinous wrong. Inspired by this principle, we legislate against abortion. But then we find that this statute does much harm and little good. Quackery and extortion are flourishing, and many women are maimed, blackmailed, or imprisoned for long periods. Great misery is thereby inflicted also upon their (partly innocent) families. All this happens even while the abortion rate is only slightly reduced below what it would be if abortion were legal.

Cohen has an easy answer to this case: The principle in question is presumably not the only ultimate principle. While it supports outlawing abortion, other principles, sensitive to the harm this statute does, will support legalization. Taking all ultimate principles together, the balance of reasons may favour rescinding the statute. But this is unproblematic because we are merely changing a rule of regulation in light of certain facts, which 'cast normative light only by reflecting the light that fact-free first principles shine on them' (267). So we jettison the statute, but not the ultimate fact-free principle supporting it.

But now we find that our problem is not fully solved. Most doctors refuse to perform abortions, quacks are still flourishing, and blackmail is still rampant. This is so because most people are known to hold that abortion is murder and that the only reason our law does not treat it as murder is that this would be inexpedient. Though we respect the law, most of us look in horror at those who have or perform abortions. Given the facts of the world as they are, our ultimate moral principles, collectively, would be better served if we revised one of these principles so that it no longer entails that abortion is a heinous wrong.

What would Cohen say about such a case? He will say that the counterproductive effects of our commitment to a principle cannot give us reason to doubt its truth: 'to say that it's futile to subscribe to a certain fundamental principle is a category mistake: unlike instituting a rule, subscribing to a principle is not an action, but the having of a belief or an attitude' (254). Talk of a category mistake sounds intimidating. But isn't this really just another way of begging the question? If our commitments to ultimate principles ought to be based solely on 'non-practical reasons,' as Cohen affirms, then it is indeed a category mistake to adduce futility or counter-productivity against them. But this does not *support* the assertion that our commitment to ultimate principles ought to be based solely on non-practical reasons.[21]

In the case of some moral commitments, this assertion seems disputable. Let me highlight one alternative, in particular, which involves a *pragmatic* attitude to our ultimate moral commitments. According to this pragmatic attitude, our ultimate commitments should serve the values they commit us to, our being committed to these principles should be approved by them. If our principles say, for example, that happiness should be promoted and unchosen inequalities avoided, then our being committed to these principles should ideally serve these tasks. If we are committed to a set of ultimate moral principles, M, and find our factual context to be one in which a revised commitment to ultimate principles M* better serves the directives of M *and* the directives of M*, then we have reason to make this revision.

Such pragmatic revision of ultimate principles clashes with Cohen's mantra. The revision of rules of regulation, which Cohen allows, works this way: Using our ultimate principles M as the basis of assessment, we find that rules R_1 work best in context C_1 and rules R_2 work best in context C_2. We thought we were living in context C_1, but find that our world is actually in condition C_2. So we revise our rules from R_1 to R_2, without any revision in M and hence without any revision of our belief that R_1 is appropriate for C_1. The pragmatist I imagine, by contrast, advocates that we should stand ready to revise even the very foundation (or 'summit') of our morality. We should revise *any* of our ultimate principles when a commitment to it turns out to have, in the world we are in, avoidably bad effects (by the lights of all our ultimate principles). Finding ourselves in context C* rather than C, we may revise from M to M* without retaining the commitment that M holds in C (that abortion would be murder if our commitment to this principle didn't have the terrible effects it actually has). We recognize, of course, that had our context turned out to be C rather than C*, we might have had no reason to revise from M to M*. But, finding ourselves in C*, we do have such reason. So we abandon M – not merely for context C*, but altogether.

---

[21] It could be said to be true by definition of 'ultimate' that a commitment to an ultimate principle must not be revised on account of its effects. But this does not settle the substantive issue. Accepting the definition, Cohen's pragmatic opponent can say that we should have no ultimate commitments.

As such pragmatists, we would not extend our morality to all possible worlds and contexts. Doing so would obstruct the task of moral reflection: to unify and complete our moral judgments while preserving or enhancing their moral plausibility. If we limit this task to the world we are in, we can achieve more unity and a better fit with our considered judgments. If we extend this task over all possible worlds, we are likely to achieve less unity and likely also to trade off fit with our considered judgments about this world (which matters greatly) against fit with our judgments about very different worlds (which matters little). It is entirely acceptable that our moral theorizing does not cover myriad remote worlds (with regressing fetuses and such) when the resulting morality provides more coherent and intuitively plausible guidance for the decisions we do or may actually face.

The point of sketching this pragmatic attitude to principles was not to advocate it. It may be unappealing for its path-dependence and relativity, assigning objectivity not to principles but only to revisions thereof (in context C* it makes sense to revise from M to M*). My point was merely to sketch yet another way, untouched by Cohen's arguments, in which one can be clear-headedly committed to fact-sensitive principles without also being committed to fact-insensitive ones. With these ways not ruled out, Cohen's rescue mission fails. He has not shown that, if there are principles, then there are fact-insensitive principles 'at the summit of our normative convictions' (20). Failing this, the argument for his lexicographical decree – that only fact-insensitive principles deserve to be called principles of justice – does not succeed.

7

JUSTICE, INCENTIVES AND CONSTRUCTIVISM

Andrew Williams

Abstract
In *Rescuing Justice and Equality*, G. A. Cohen reiterates his critique of John Rawls's difference principle as a justification for inequality-generating incentives, and also argues that Rawls's ambition to provide a constructivist defence of the first principles of justice is doomed. Cohen's arguments also suggest a natural response to my earlier attempt to defend the basic structure objection to Cohen's critique, which I term the alien factors reply. This essay criticises the reply, and Cohen's more general argument against Rawls's constructivism.[1]

I. Introduction

This essay examines some issues arising from my earlier reply to G. A. Cohen's critique of John Rawls's version of the incentive argument for economic inequality.[2]

As a preliminary, and to illustrate the Rawlsian incentive argument and Cohen's critique, imagine a society where occupations are allocated via a competitive labour market, inequality-generating incentives are prohibited, and workers with unequal endowments of productive talents choose which occupations to pursue on the basis of job satisfaction. Suppose the society initially has an equal distribution of income and wealth – e.g. (D1) 100, 100, 100 – but that everyone's level of advantage would be improved if inequality-generating incentives were permitted,

[1] For very helpful discussion, I am grateful to Chris Bertram, Paula Casal, Tom Christiano, Matthew Clayton, G. A. Cohen, Ronald Dworkin, Brian Feltham, Brad Hooker, Rahul Kumar, Jimmy Lenman, Thomas Pogge, Lukas Meyer, Michael Otsuka, Adam Swift, Victor Tadros, and audiences at Berne, Bristol, University College London, Queen's, Sheffield, and Sussex. I also gratefully acknowledge funding provided by award B/IA/112990 from the Arts and Humanities Research Council.
[2] See Andrew Williams, 'Incentives, Inequality, and Publicity', *Philosophy and Public Affairs*, 27 (1998), pp. 225–247, which responds to criticisms reprinted, with some additions, in G. A. Cohen, *Rescuing Justice and Equality* (Cambridge, M.A.: Harvard University Press, 2008), chs. 1–3.

thereby modifying workers' productive decision-making. The argument then claims that if an unequal distribution – e.g. (D2) 200, 400, 800 – satisfies lexically prior principles of justice, including ones protecting basic civil liberties and fair equality of opportunity, and is not detrimental to the least advantaged relative to any feasible alternative, then the inequality it contains does not make it unjust.

In response, and amongst others things, Cohen has claimed that the incentive argument mistakenly assumes that justice places no moral limits on mutually disinterested market behaviour, and as a result permits too many inequalities. Instead, the Rawlsian argument's concern to share the effects of social and natural fortune is better expressed by a *strict* difference principle, applying to workers' productive decisions as well as public policies, than by a *lax* difference principle, applying only to the latter. If workers accept the strict principle, however, an *egalitarian ethos* will govern individuals' decisions in the labour market, and another efficient but more equal distribution – e.g. (D3) 400, 450, 500 – would be feasible without relying on as extensive inequality-generating incentives as those in (D2). If so, then (D2) is detrimental to the least advantaged, and so Rawlsians should regard it as less just than (D3).

To elaborate some of the details of Cohen's position, suppose that everyone does initially uphold the egalitarian ethos, and (D3) is achieved. The most talented amongst us then lose their commitment, and are no longer willing to work as productively unless they receive 800 rather than a mere 500 units reward. Since the egalitarian ethos is sensitive to *labour burdens* and to the distinction between *intention-dependent* and *intention-independent* inequalities, and grants workers an *agent-centred prerogative* to be self-serving to some reasonable degree, we then ask them the following questions.

(i)   Have your jobs become so *onerous* that you would be worse off than others unless you received 800 units?
(ii) Is it *too difficult* for you to work as hard at 500 as at 800 units?
(iii) Is unreasonable to expect you to work as hard at 500 as at 800 units because it would be *so costly* for you to do so?

Answering us, they say 'No' to all our questions. Having voted, we implement (D2), but we also ask ourselves the following.

(iv) Have we acquiesced in the face of some individuals' failure to act justly?

(v) Have we implemented a distribution that is, in at least one important respect, unjust?

Cohen's critique implies that the answer to both our questions is 'Yes'. How then might advocates of the incentive argument reply to the critique?

Various replies are possible, one of which claims the critique overlooks the restricted scope of Rawls's principles of justice. Suggesting what Cohen terms the *basic structure objection*, Rawls himself emphasizes that

> the principles of justice, in particular the difference principle, apply to the main public principles and policies that regulate social and economic inequalities. . . The difference principle holds, for example, for income and property taxation, for fiscal and economic policy. It applies to the announced system of public law and statutes and not to particular transactions or distributions, nor to the decisions of individuals and associa- tions, but rather to the institutional background against which these transactions and decisions take place.[3]

According to the basic structure objection, there is an important discontinuity in the moral reasons that apply to the design and maintenance of fundamental institutions and those that apply to decisions within those institutions. Since the difference principle does not apply to the latter decisions, Cohen is mistaken to claim that Rawls's position must favour the strict over the lax version of the difference principle, and so require workers to embrace an egalitarian ethos that renders redundant many of the inequality- generating incentives justified by the incentive argument.

Unconvinced by this objection, Cohen has argued that those who appeal to the restricted scope of the difference principles fall prey to a dilemma. Depending on how they define the basic structure, advocates of the objection

> must either admit application of the principles of justice to (legally optional) social practices, and, indeed, to patterns of

---

[3]   John Rawls, *Political Liberalism* (New York: Columbia University Press, 1993), pp. 282–83.

personal choice that are not legally prescribed, both because they are the substance of those practices, and because they are similarly profound in effect, *in which case the restriction of justice to* [the basic – AW] *structure, in any sense collapses*; or, if he restricts his concern to the coercive structure only, then *he saddles himself with a purely arbitrary delineation of his subject matter.*[4]

Cohen argues, roughly, that advocates of the basic structure objection have two options. Taking the first option, they can adopt a broad understanding of the basic structure, encompassing *all* activity that exerts profound and unavoidable effects on individuals' lives. But in that case their attempt to restrict the scope of Rawlsian distributive principles *collapses* since the activities of incentive-takers are no less part of the basic structure than those who uphold the egalitarian ethos. Taking the second option, they may instead adopt a narrow understanding of the basic structure in terms of legally coercive institutions. Given this construal, however, the restriction is *arbitrary*, since undefended, and *implausible*, since it renders various forms of injustice within the family immune to criticism by appeal to those principles.

My earlier reply offered a version of the basic structure objection designed to escape Cohen's dilemma by showing that the options it considers are non-exhaustive. To do so, I attempted to show that none of Cohen's charges applied to a third conception of the basic structure as extending beyond legally coercive institutions but excluding influential activities incapable of regulation by public rules.

Turning first to the implausibility charge, I accepted Cohen's claim that examples of gender injustice within the family show that restricting Rawls's principles is plausible only if the basic structure extends beyond the legal order. Even so, I claimed that there are still grounds to resist its expansion to encompass occupational decision-making whenever it exerts profound influence. Identifying those grounds, I explained how Rawls defines the basic structure by reference not only to its disposition to produce profound and unavoidable effects but also to its possession of certain additional formal properties.

Having denied that those formal properties depended on the basic structure comprising only legal rules, I instead appealed to

---

[4] G. A. Cohen, *Rescuing Justice and Equality*, p. 137, italics added.

Rawls's description of the basic structure as 'the *institutional* background against which these transactions and decisions take place'.[5] Given Rawls's definition of an 'institution' as 'a *public system of rules* which defines offices and positions with their rights and duties, powers and immunities, and the like',[6] along with his remarks about various publicity requirements rules might satisfy,[7] I then concluded the basic structure is better characterized as the concrete expression of a set of profoundly influential rules, conformity with which is sufficiently verifiable by shared methods of enquiry.

Armed with this characterization, in order to address Cohen's charge of arbitrariness I suggested that if Rawls is correct to assume that it is desirable for principles of social justice to be capable of facilitating *well-ordered social cooperation* then there are reasons to construe the basic structure as encompassing only those influential activities that conform with, or violate, certain *public rules.* Finally, addressing the collapse charge, I appealed to the difficulty of verifying answers to questions like (i), (ii), and (iii) in order to show that Cohen's egalitarian ethos, unlike a gender egalitarian domestic ethos, is not sufficiently public for it to qualify as part of the basic structure, and thus as required by Rawls's distributive principles

By drawing attention to Rawls's assumptions about the value of well-ordered social cooperation, and the significance of the fact of limited information, I aimed to show that his attitude to inequality-generating incentives coheres with some of his deeper but less obvious commitments,[8] and is to at least some degree plausible. I also recognized, however, that various additional objections remained unanswered.[9] These included revised forms of the implausibility and collapse charges, as well as a fresh charge, designed to pre-empt appeal to publicity in debates about *justice* without challenging its relevance to debates about other

[5]   John Rawls, *Political Liberalism,* p. 283.
[6]   John Rawls, *A Theory of Justice,* Revised Edition (Cambridge, M.A.: Harvard University Press, 1999) pp. 47–48.
[7]   See Rawls, *A Theory of Justice,* pp. 48–49, and *Political Liberalism,* pp. 66–67.
[8]   Thus, I concluded that 'Cohen has not produced a purely internal critique of the Rawlsian defense of inequality-generating incentives. The impression that he has done so depends . . . upon overlooking the fundamental role that the ideal of a well-ordered society plays within Rawls's thought.' ('Incentives, Inequality, and Publicity', p. 246)
[9]   Thus, I wrote that some 'might regard the ideal [of well-ordered social cooperation] as either unsound or irrelevant to the choice between competing conceptions of *justice.* They will infer that my restatement, even if not arbitrary, is still implausible.' Ibid.

types of moral principle. In this essay I turn to the fresh charge, which I now label the *alien factors reply*.[10] To do so, I focus on the version suggested by Cohen's thought-provoking new work, *Rescuing Justice and Equality*.

II. The alien factors reply

Cohen's version of the alien factors reply involves a distinction between 'rules of regulation' and 'fundamental principles of justice'.[11] The contrast between these two types of moral norm proceeds along two dimensions. First, offering some explanation of the distinction between rules of regulation and fundamental principles in general, Cohen states that 'a rule of regulation is "a device for having certain effects", which we adopt or not, in the light of an evaluation, precisely, of its likely effects, and, therefore, in the light of an understanding of the facts. And we evaluate those effects, and thereby decide which fact-bound principles to adopt, by reference to principles that are not devices for achieving effects but statements of our more ultimate and fact-free convictions.'[12] Second, Cohen explains that he adds 'to the distinction between fundamental principles and rules of regulation a simpler distinction between justice and other virtues, and, therefore, between (c) principles that express or serve the value of justice and (d) principles that express or serve other values, such as human welfare, or human self-realization, or the promotion of knowledge.'[13]

We can summarise these remarks by noting that rules of regulation are less *robust* than fundamental principles because their justification is instrumental, and therefore always depends on the truth of contingent empirical assumptions about the consequences of individuals accepting such rules; in sharp contrast, the justification of fundamental principles never depends on such truths. In addition, rules of regulation are less *pure* than principles of justice since the former may answer to a plurality of values whereas the

[10]   The label is suggested by Cohen's remark that 'the influence of alien factors on the output of the constructivist procedure means that what it produces is not fundamental justice. . . .' See *Rescuing Justice and Equality*, p. 284.

[11]   For various remarks about the distinction, see *Rescuing Justice and Equality*, pp. 253–54, 263–272, and 274–79.

[12]   See *Rescuing Justice and Equality*, p. 265, quoting from Robert Nozick, *The Nature of Rationality* (Princeton: Princeton University Press, 1993), p. 38.

[13]   See *Rescuing Justice and Equality*, p. 277.

latter answer only to one distinctive value, namely justice. How then does the contrast figure in the alien factors argument?

When reconstructed as a critique to my earlier effort to resurrect the basic structure objection, the reply proceeds as follows.

   (i) Rawls's theory of justice claims that inequality-generating incentives can satisfy fundamental principles of distributive justice.

  (ii) The justification of fundamental principles does not depend upon the truth of any contingent factual assumptions.

 (iii) The justification of fundamental principles of justice does not appeal to any requirements unrelated to justice.

 (iv) According to the revised basic structure objection, the justification of distributive principles depends on various contingent factual assumptions about limited information, and the degree to which such principles satisfy publicity requirements.

  (v) The requirements of distributive justice and of publicity are unrelated.

 (vi) The revised objection can be used only as a defence of rules of regulation and not of fundamental principles of justice.

Therefore,

The revised objection cannot vindicate Rawls's claim that inequality-generating incentives can satisfy first principles of justice.

If the above version of the alien factors argument succeeds, the revised basic structure objection is doomed to fail as a means of showing that inequality-generating incentives can be fully just.

Worse still, at least for Rawlsians, Cohen's work also suggests that a more general problem threatens Rawls's theory of justice. Thus, Cohen argues that the revised basic structure objection is a manifestation of the constructivist method Rawls employs to pursue his aim of justifying a set of fundamental principles of justice. There is, however, a deep incoherence between Rawls's ambition to devise a plausible theory of justice and the constructivist method by which he pursues it. The incoherence arises because Rawls's favoured constructive procedure, his famous *origi-*

nal position argument, allows the justification of his principles to depend on factual contingencies (e.g. limited information) and values unrelated to justice (e.g. stability and publicity). Yet even if such a procedure does succeed in justifying some plausible rules of regulation it is bound to fail to identify norms that are sufficiently robust and pure to qualify as fundamental principles of justice. Thus, Cohen concludes that his 'distinction between ultimate fact-free principles and adopted rules of regulation . . . refutes Rawlsian constructivism as a meta-theory of justice'.[14] How then might Rawlsians, and advocates of the revised basic structure objection, respond?

I now examine one natural line of argument against the alien factors reply. My response accepts Cohen's claim that Rawls's own constructive procedure fails to ground fundamental principles of justice in the relevantly robust and pure sense but denies Cohen's allegation that Rawls's principles amount to mere rules of regulation. Instead the distinction between rules of regulation and fundamental principles of justice is non-exhaustive, and Rawls's ambition to identify the first principles of social justice is best understood in rather different terms. Accurately understood, there is no conflict between his ambition and his constructivist method. There is also no need to deny the validity of other types of principles justified in distinct ways, including robust and pure principles of justice in Cohen's sense.

III. Rawlsian constructivism

Since philosophers interpret constructivism in very different ways it is worth beginning by stating the sense in which I understand

---

[14] See *Rescuing Justice and Equality*, p. 269; see also p. 283, where Cohen describes 'the general ground of my disagreement with the constructivist meta-theory' as follows: 'in any enterprise whose purpose is to select the principles that I have called "rules of regulation", *attention must be paid, either expressly or in effect, to considerations that do not reflect the content of justice itself*: while justice . . . must of course influence the selection of regulating principles, factual contingencies that determine how justice is to be applied, or that make justice infeasible, *and* values and principles that call for a compromise with justice, also have a role to play in generating the principles that regulate social life, and legislators . . . will go astray unless they are influenced . . . by those further considerations. It follows that any procedure that generates the right set of principles to regulate society fails thereby to identify a set of fundamental principles of justice, by virtue of its very success in the former, distinct, exercise. The influence of other values means that the principles in the output of the procedure are not principles of *justice*, and the influence of the factual contingencies means that they are not *fundamental* principles of anything.'

Rawls's conception of justice as fairness to be a version of constructivism. Constructivism in this sense is a doctrine within
normative ethics, which offers a distinctive explanation of why
certain facts provide sound reasons to affirm certain substantive
moral or political judgments.[15] More specifically, a constructivist
explanation characteristically proceeds by appealing to certain
principles that pass some procedural test, and thereby not
merely summarise which facts are reason-giving but actually help
confer that status upon them. A constructivist theory of justice
therefore indentifies which properties of acts or institutions
make them just or unjust, and appeals to certain procedurally
justified principles as grounds for belief in those properties'
justice-making status.

Rawls implicitly endorses a constructivist explanation of judgments of social justice in *A Theory of Justice* when he claims 'the
moral facts [i.e. facts that provide reasons to affirm that specific
institutions are just or unjust] are determined by the principles
which would be chosen in the original position. These principles
specify which considerations are relevant from the standpoint of
social justice.'[16] The doctrine is explicitly stated in his later work,
and most boldly so in his Dewey Lectures, where Rawls claims
that an

> essential feature of a constructivist view, as illustrated by justice
> as fairness, is that its first principles single out what facts its
> citizens are to count as reasons of justice. Apart from the pro-
> cedure of constructing these principles, there are no reasons of
> justice and what their relative force is can be ascertained only
> on the basis of principles that result from the construction.[17]

It is worth noting, however, that it is far from obvious that the very
idea of justifying certain normative principles by showing that they
would emerge from some suitably described selection procedure

---

[15] In Cohen's terms, I favour 'a view according to which the constructivist procedure
merely *makes* the principles valid, but . . . does not say that their-having-been-produced-by-
the-favoured-procedure is what it *is* for them to be valid.' See *Rescuing Justice and Equality*,
pp. 275–76.

[16] See *A Theory of Justice*, p. 40.

[17] See John Rawls, 'Kantian Constructivism in Moral Theory', Samuel Freeman (ed.),
John Rawls: Collected Papers (Cambridge: Harvard University Press, 1999), p. 351. See also
Political Liberalism, Lecture III, for Rawls's eventual more qualified *political constructivism*
and its relationship to Kant's *moral constructivism*.

precludes justifying robust and pure principles of justice. The selectors might, for example, be deprived of contingent factual information, and be instructed to choose amongst some complex conditional principles that favour certain responses if various different facts obtain.[18] Their motivation might also be purified so that they attach no importance to at least some of those considerations Cohen insists are irrelevant in identifying the distinctive demands of justice. To understand why justice as fairness fails to deliver robust and pure principles we should, therefore, attend to the details of the particular constructive procedure Rawls employs.

Here it is particularly relevant to our discussion of incentives to recall that Rawls's original position argument tests rival principles, in part, by focusing on a principle's capacity to play what he terms a particular *social role*, namely that of facilitating well-ordered social cooperation between the individuals to whom it applies. Rawls also clearly acknowledges that a principle's success in performing its role depends on contingent facts about limited information, which sometimes favour choosing simpler or more restricted principles than might otherwise be the case. As he explains,

> the limitations that affect our moral deliberations affect the requirements of publicity and support the use of priority rules. These limitations also lead us to take the basic structure of a well-ordered society as the first subject of justice and to adopt the primary goods as the basis of interpersonal comparison . . .[19]

Rawls's elaboration of this thought shows that his particular form of constructivism clearly bears on whether the difference principle supports an incentive argument for inequality. Thus, he writes that a

> moral conception is to have a wide social role as part of public culture . . . Now if it is to play this wide role, a conception's first principles cannot be so complex that they cannot be generally understood and followed in the more important cases. Thus,

---

[18]   For relevant discussion, see G. A. Cohen's treatment of 'factless constructivism' (p. 300) in *Rescuing Justice and Equality*, pp. 298–300. At p. 299 Cohen contrasts the Rawslian version of constructivism with a more general version in which 'selectors are deprived of the information with which actually existing constructivisms about justice endow them. They would then produce rules of regulation for each possible world, or set of assumptions about the facts, which they can reach by formulating principled reactions to merely *hypothesized facts.*'

[19]   See Rawls, 'Kantian Constructivism in Moral Theory', p. 347.

it is desirable that knowing whether these principles are satisfied, at least with reference to fundamental liberties and basic institutions, should not depend on information difficult to obtain or hard to evaluate. To incorporate these desiderata in a constructivist view, the parties are assumed to take these considerations into account and to prefer (other things equal) principles that are easy to understand and simple to apply. The gain in compliance and willing acceptance by citizens more than makes up for the rough and ready nature of the guiding framework that results and its neglect of certain distinctions and differences. In effect, the parties agree to rule out certain facts as irrelevant in questions of justice concerning the basic structure, even though they recognize that in regard to other cases it may be appropriate to appeal to them. From the standpoint of the original position, eliminating these facts as reasons of social justice sufficiently increases the capacity of the conception to fulfill its social role.[20]

There is then considerable evidence for Cohen's claim that the constructivist dimension of justice as fairness implies that its principles, including the incentive-friendly lax difference principle, are not fundamental principles of justice in the robust and pure sense Cohen has in mind.[21]

It would, however, be an invalid inference to an unsound conclusion to affirm Cohen's additional claim that Rawls's principles of justice amount merely to rules of regulation. The inference fails because, as Cohen recognises,[22] the distinction between fundamental principles of justice and rules of regulation that serve justice does not exhaust the range of conceivable principles of justice. According to constructivism, as I have explained, there are fact-sensitive principles that are not mere instruments.

[20] See Rawls, 'Kantian Constructivism in Moral Theory', p. 347.

[21] Note that the demands of Cohen's own egalitarian ethos are also fact-sensitive since they vary depending on contingent psychological assumptions about the extent to which workers are unable rather than merely unwilling to produce without inequality-generating incentives. Some might also insist the agent-centred prerogative present in the ethos does not modify the demands of justice but is instead an alien factor that renders it morally permissible to fail to meet those demands. Thus, Cohen's account of fundamental principles of justice suggests that even if a society lives up to his egalitarian ethos it may not satisfy such principles.

[22] See *Rescuing Justice and Equality*, p. 276, where Cohen notes that the distinction between fundamental normative principles and rules of regulation 'is not exhaustive because there exist derivative normative principles, some fact-insensitive and some not, which are not rules of regulation.'

More importantly, the conclusion is unsound because rules of regulation, as Cohen characterises them, are necessarily objects of choice, which individuals, or groups, adopt as means to serve other more fundamental principles by, for instance, enhancing conformity with their demands. According to Rawls's constructivism, however, his first principles of justice are optional *only* for the imaginary agents involved in the constructive procedure. For non-imaginary agents like ourselves, or agents in a society governed by justice as fairness, the hypothetical choices of those imaginary agents are supposed to provide sound reasons to believe in the validity of those non-robust and impure principles, and the judgements they support about the facts that make institutions just or unjust.[23] In addition, as my previous account of Rawls's view indicated, whilst his principles are fact-sensitive they are not justified solely as instruments to enhance conformity with reasons of justice whose validity is prior to those principles.[24] Instead the principles are prior to those reasons in the sense that they supply grounds to affirm that certain facts are reasons of justice.

If the idea of rules of regulation does illuminate Rawls's view, then it is better employed to describe the social institutions, or public systems of rules, that his principles of justice are designed to assess and not those principles themselves. Here much will depend on how the idea of rules of regulation is elaborated, an issue I shall not address.[25] Even without doing this, however, I hope to have cast some doubt on Cohen's charge that 'it is a fundamental error of *A Theory of Justice* that it identifies the first principles of justice with the principles that we should adopt to regulate society.'[26] It is a further issue, to which we now turn, whether the alien factors reply succeeds.

---

[23] Here I follow 'Kantian Constructivism in Moral Theory', p. 320, where Rawls points out the need 'to distinguish three points of view: that of the parties in the original position, that of citizens in a well-ordered society, and finally, that of ourselves – you and me – who are examining justice as fairness . . .'

[24] See the contrast Rawls draws between classical utilitarianism and justice as fairness, and between 'rules and precepts' and 'first principles', in 'Kantian Constructivism and Moral Theory', pp. 351–52.

[25] For example, are optimal rules of regulation norms that individuals should always conform with rather than merely adopt? Perhaps Cohen's reference to living by rules (p. 275) suggests an affirmative answer but see *Rescuing Justice and Equality*, p. 270, which introduces a gap between 'what to do' and 'what would be the right rule to adopt'.

[26] See *Rescuing Justice and Equality*, p. 265, and cp. p. 277.

IV. 'First principles of justice'

The success of the alien factors reply depends, in large part, on whether justice as fairness either aims to defend fundamental principles of justice in Cohen's sense, or needs to do so. Turning first to the interpretive issue, I shall now argue that Cohen's assumption about constructivism's 'aspiration to produce fundamental principles of justice' is implausible.[27]

As a preliminary, recall Sidgwick's remarks about the difficulty in defining 'common moral terms', according to which 'there is no case where the difficulty is greater, or the result more disputed, than when we try to define Justice.'[28] The remarks suggest to me that although Rawls and Cohen both use the same terminology, we should not be very surprised if they understand the idea of a fundamental principle of justice, or phrase 'first principles of justice', quite differently. Rawls's own remarks also support this suspicion. For example, stating explicitly that the first principles of his theory are not robust in the sense mentioned above, Rawls writes that

> in justice as fairness the first principles of justice depend upon those general beliefs of about human nature and how society works which are allowed to the parties in the original position. First principles are not, in a constructivist view, independent of such beliefs, nor, as some forms of rational intuitionism hold, true in all possible worlds.[29]

If Rawls shared Cohen's understanding of 'first principles of justice', then the remark involves an error that is likely to have been apparent to its author. Interpretative charity, therefore, counts against Cohen's assumptions about Rawls's ambitions, and premise (i) in my earlier reconstruction of his argument.

Some of Rawls's remarks at the start of *A Theory of Justice* about the subject matter of his theory provide even more counter-evidence to Cohen's assumption. Here Rawls explains at some length how he will construe the idea of principles of justice, and does so by remarking about such principles' stringency, role, and grounds.

[27] See *Rescuing Justice and Equality*, p. 284.
[28] See Henry Sidgwick, *Methods of Ethics*, Seventh Edition (London: Macmillan, 1962), IIII.V.1, p. 264.
[29] See Rawls, 'Kantian Constructivism in Moral Theory', p. 351.

Appealing to 'our intuitive conviction of the primacy of justice,'[30] Rawls begins by proclaiming justice to be 'the first virtue of social institutions, as truth is of systems of thought', and insisting that 'laws and institutions no matter how efficient and well-arranged must be reformed or abolished if they are unjust'.[31] Here I assume that Rawls' reference to the constitutive relationship between thought and truth indicates that he is expressing a conceptual claim about standards of justice, comparable to the claim that sound moral standards necessarily override non-moral standards.[32] Thus, his remarks suggest that, at the very least, whenever conflict arises, any reasons provided by sound principles of justice necessarily defeat a range of weighty conflicting reasons. The alien factors reply, however, does not specify the degree of stringency that sound first principles of justice necessarily possess, and so may be consistent with this aspect of Rawls's understanding of the principles.

It is far less clear that proponents of the reply can accommodate Rawls's other remarks since these strongly suggest that on his understanding first principles of justice need not be pure. Thus, Rawls states that he takes 'the concept of justice . . . to be defined . . . by the role of its principles in assigning rights and duties and in defining the appropriate division of social advantages.'[33] This statement is immediately preceded by the claim that 'any reasonably complete ethical theory must include principles for this fundamental problem and that these principles, *whatever they are*, constitute its doctrine of justice.'[34] Both remarks show that on Rawls's understanding, unlike Cohen's, there is no conceptual bar on grounding what he terms 'first principles of justice' in a plurality of values. Rawls confirms this impression when he notes that a variety of effects that they might produce can justify principles of justice. Thus, referring to its consequences for 'efficiency' and 'stability', he claims that we 'cannot, in general, assess a conception of justice by its distributive role alone, however useful this role may be in identifying the concept of justice . . . We

[30] See *A Theory of Justice*, p. 4.
[31] See *A Theory of Justice*, p. 3.
[32] For a different reading of Rawls as stating a substantive rather than conceptual claim about the stringency of justice, see Cohen, *Rescuing Justice and Equality*, pp. 302–306, esp. p. 305.
[33] *A Theory of Justice*, p. 9.
[34] *A Theory of Justice*, p. 9, italics added.

must take into account its wider connections . . . *other things equal, one conception of justice is preferable to another when its broader consequences are more desirable.*'[35]

I conclude then that Rawls's remarks, and in particular his claims about a conception of justice's 'broader consequences' enhancing its plausibility, show that although Rawls employs similar terminology he does not aim to identify first principles of justice in Cohen's robust and pure sense.

Proponents of the revised basic structure objection can undermine the alien factors reply by appealing to this conclusion. We can argue that Rawls's version of the incentive argument claims only that certain stringent though non-robust and impure distributive principles permit inequality-generating incentives, such as those present in (D2). An appeal to facts about limited information and publicity requirements may suffice to explain why those principles have limited scope, and can be satisfied in the absence of an egalitarian ethos. Those who criticize such an appeal as irrelevant to the question of whether justice in some more robust and pure sense favours (D3) rather than (D2) *are not addressing the incentive argument's main claim.* Moreover, their accusation that Rawls's theory of justice is incoherent because of the incompatibility between it aims and its constructivist method also appears much less plausible once we realize that Rawls does not aim to justify any first principles of justice in Cohen's sense.

V. Reconciliation?

The previous reply is to some degree conciliatory insofar as it suggests that Rawls and Cohen are addressing different questions.[36] Thus, Rawls aims to identify a set of stringent principles grounded on a plurality of values and set of factual assumptions that can guide us in designing and maintaining our most profoundly influential social institutions. Given the conclusive

---

[35] *A Theory of Justice*, p. 6.

[36] Cp. T. M. Scanlon's sapient observation that when Rawls and Cohen discuss compensation for individuals with relatively expensive tastes there is 'some reason to think that they are not always talking about the same thing' and that this 'makes it more difficult than one might have expected to be clear about the exact nature of their disagreement.' See T. M. Scanlon, 'Justice, Responsibility, and the Demands of Equality', Christine Sypnowich (ed.), *The Egalitarian Conscience – Essays in Honour of G. A. Cohen* (Oxford: Oxford University Press, 2006), p. 85.

character of those principles, and the significance of their subject-matter, the philosophical and political importance of Rawls's ambition is clear.[37] Once we also recognize that Rawls's principles are not mere rules of regulation, it then becomes far less clear how Cohen can plausibly respond to the question he himself poses, namely 'if Rawls hadn't called his principles "principles of justice", would you then have no quarrel with him?'[38]

In sharp contrast, Cohen's aim is more difficult to characterize than Rawls's aim. Such a difficulty arises in part because Cohen devotes less attention than Rawls to specifying his understanding of justice, and instead explains his aim largely in opposition to Rawls. We are told, for example, that justice in the fundamental sense that preoccupies Cohen is independent of facts, and only one of a plurality of values unrelated to publicity and even pareto efficiency. At least for me, however, the precise question that Cohen is addressing remains far more elusive than Rawls's question.[39]

Nevertheless, a critic might object to the previous reply by arguing it concedes that Rawls's theory is importantly incomplete insofar it fails to answer some questions that could intelligibly be claimed to concern distributive justice. Many of us have convictions about how to rank different distributions of benefits and burdens between individuals abstracting from any practical limitations whatsoever, including the extent to which those distributions fall within any agent's control. We might, for example, endorse a telic egalitarian distributive principle that implies a world in which some are sighted and some blind is less than fully just even if such inequality was undetectable

---

[37] Having understood what Rawls means by 'justice', suppose that some readers of *A Theory of Justice* who use the term 'justice' in the same sense as Cohen, then realise that Rawls has, as Cohen puts it, 'provided a theory of something, well, *sort* of like justice'. It seems to me that their sense of 'excitement' at Rawls's achievement should then increase rather than diminish. See *Rescuing Justice and Equality*, p. 304.

[38] See *Rescuing Justice from Equality*, p. 304. Note that like his response to critics 'who ask, dismissively, "What's in a name?"', Cohen's suggestion that Rawls is not engaged in an enquiry about 'an elusive virtue discussed for a few thousand years by philosophers' (p. 304), relies heavily on the assumption that Rawls's principles are rules of regulation.

[39] As he anticipates, Cohen's reference to 'the ancient dictum that justice is giving each person her due' in order to 'say what I think justice is, in general terms', fails to solve the problem. See Cohen, *Rescuing Justice and Equality*, p. 7, and pp. 252–53, where Cohen suggests that if 'justice is, as Justinian said, each person getting her due, then justice is her due irrespective of the constraints that might make it impossible to give it to her.'

and unavoidable.[40] It is conceivable that it is this type of distribution-sensitive axiological principle that Cohen has in mind when referring to first principles of justice.

It is not clear to me, however, why recognizing the limited ambitions of Rawls's theory weakens the theory rather than strengthens it by making it less vulnerable to apparent counter-examples. In the case just mentioned, for example, its advocates can point out that the term 'justice' is ambiguous in ordinary language, and concede that there may be some sense in which unavoidable inequality is 'unjust', whilst denying that the theory addresses questions about justice in that sense, or that answers to those questions are obviously relevant elsewhere. Following Rawls's observation that

> the exclusion of . . . facts as reasons of social justice does not alone entail that they are not reasons in other kinds of situation where different moral notions apply. Indeed it is not even ruled out that the account of some notions should be constructivist, whereas the account of others is not.[41]

they might even allow that some sound robust and pure first principles do rank (D3) above (D2), but because of practical limits still insist that this does not suffice to establish even a *pro tanto* requirement for workers to try to establish (D3) through their occupational choices or wage negotiations.

VI. Conclusion

Rescuing Justice and Equality contains a barrage of ingenious challenges to the Rawlsian incentive argument for inequality. Even if Rawls's constructivism and my own attempt to defend the basic structure argument, withstand the charges I have canvassed here, Cohen still has a daunting array of additional arguments that I have not yet mentioned let alone properly addressed. Thanks to Cohen's latest work the need for liberal egalitarians to engage in sustained discussion of them is inescapable.

[40]   See Derek Parfit, 'Equality or Priority?', Matthew Clayton and Andrew Williams (eds.), *The Ideal of Equality* (Basingstoke: Macmillan, 2001) for further discussion of the distinction between *telic* and *deontic* egalitarianism. To mention another widespread conviction about retributive justice, many of us also think that there is some sense in which injustice exists when the innocent are punished even if the imposition of such punishment was reasonably unavoidable, and the best institutions are in place and meet with full compliance.

[41]   See Rawls, 'Kantian Constructivism in Moral Theory', p. 348.

INDEX

Printed and bound by CPI Group (UK) Ltd, Croydon, CR0 4YY

13/04/2025

14656464-0001